Series / Number 07-003

# CAUSAL MODELING

**HERBERT B. ASHER**
*Ohio State University*

**SAGE PUBLICATIONS** / Beverly Hills / London

*For information address:*

SAGE PUBLICATIONS, INC.
275 South Beverly Drive
Beverly Hills, California 90212

SAGE PUBLICATIONS LTD
St George's House / 44 Hatton Garden
London EC1N 8ER

International Standard Book Number 0-8039-0654-4

Library of Congress Catalog Card No. L.C. 76-25696

SECOND PRINTING

---

When citing a University Paper, please use the proper form. Remember to cite the
correct Sage University Paper series title and include the paper number. One of the
two following formats can be adapted (depending on the style manual used):

(1) IVERSEN, GUDMUND R. and NORPOTH, HELMUT (1976) "Analysis of
Variance." Sage University Paper series on Quantitative Applications in the Social
Sciences, 07-001. Beverly Hills and London: Sage Pubns.

*OR*

(2) Iversen, Gudmund R. and Norpoth, Helmut. 1976. *Analysis of Variance.* Sage
University Paper series on Quantitative Applications in the Social Sciences, series no.
07-001. Beverly Hills and London: Sage Publications.

# CONTENTS

HERBERT B. ASHER, *associate professor of political science at the Ohio State University, received his B.S. degree from Bucknell University and his Ph.D. from the University of Michigan. He is the author of* Presidential Elections and American Politics: Voters, Candidates, and Campaigns Since 1952 *(1976), as well as numerous articles on legislative politics and political behavior methodology. Dr. Asher is also the author of* Freshman Representatives and the Learning of Voting Cues *(1973) and coauthor of* Determinants of Public Welfare Policies *(1973), both publications of Sage Professional Papers in American Politics.*

# Editor's Introduction

CAUSAL MODELING attempts to resolve questions about possible *causes*—providing explanations of phenomena (effects) as the result of previous phenomena (causes). CAUSAL MODELING is a technique for selecting those variables that are potential determinants of the effects—and then attempting to isolate the separate contributions to the effects made by each cause (predictor variable).

However, the technique of CAUSAL MODELING cannot establish causal implications as philosophers conceptualize it: "that because of which something is or becomes" or "anything responsible for change, motion, or action." No statistical technique can deal with "final causes" because the nature and limitations inherent in CAUSAL MODELING are those of any inexact, nondeterministic, and flexible model. But there are many things that properly applied CAUSAL MODELING can do:

- A political scientist might try to determine whether a congressman's voting behavior is caused by his personal beliefs and attitudes, or by his expectations of constituent attitudes. But if both are determinants of the congressman's actions, then it would be appropriate to assay the impact of each determinant upon the other, while controlling for the congressman's perceptions of constituency attitudes in forming his own reaction to legislation.

- An economist can use this technique to examine the causes of unemployment or inflation, with wage rates and alternative levels of government expenditures considered as potential causal factors.

- A sociologist might try to determine whether an adolescent's vocational aspirations are caused by his level of education or his parents' career achievements, or by his socioeconomic environment and peers' expectations. And if each of these is a determinant, then it would be useful to assess the impact of each, as well as the reverse implications—for example, do his career aspirations affect his peers' attitudes or modify his level of educational attainment?

- An educator or psychologist might use this tool to determine whether scores on standard intelligence or achievement tests are—if fact—causally related to ethnicity or sex or level of education, with characteristics of the students' environment serving as possible intervening factors. (The best-known example of this application is the famous or infamous report by Christopher Jencks.*)

Such examples do not encompass the full range of social scientific inquiry that can be explored with CAUSAL MODELING. For example, in this paper CAUSAL MODELING is illustrated with examples from political socialization studies and congressional voting patterns, reflecting the particular interests of the author. Herbert Asher develops the basic concepts behind causal modeling, presuming some general understanding of correlation and the fundamental concepts of regression analysis.** His explication includes a discussion of path analysis (a technique developed by the geneticist, Sewall Wright), multiple indicators,*** and an explanation of spurious correlation—a relationship between two variables that are not causally interrelated, although they may at first appear to be. The concepts and techniques offered are applicable to most living teleological (that is, purposeful) system—including influence and power relations—as well as to inanimate relationships across the spectrum of the social sciences.

—E. M. Uslaner, Series Editor

*Christopher Jencks (1973) *Inequality: A Reassessment of the Effect of Family and Schooling in America.* New York: Harper & Row.

**For an introduction to these techniques, readers may consult two papers within this series: Eric Uslaner (forthcoming) *Regression Analysis: Simultaneous Equation Estimation* and Charles Ostrom (forthcoming) *Regression Analysis: Time Series Analysis,* both in the Sage University Papers in Quantitative Applications in the Social Sciences. Beverly Hills and London: Sage Publications.

***For a related dicussion of this topic, readers may obtain another paper in this series: John L. Sullivan (forthcoming) *Multiple Indicators.* Sage University Papers in Quantitative Applications in the Social Sciences. Beverly Hills and London: Sage Publications.

# CAUSAL MODELING

**HERBERT B. ASHER**
*Ohio State University*

## 1. INTRODUCTION

### OVERVIEW

**Causal modeling has become an increasingly popular** heuristic and analytic tool with social scientists. Our primary concern in this paper is with the set of causal analysis techniques appropriate for interval data, although relaxations of the interval requirement will be considered. The techniques to be discussed range from correlational tests for spurious relationships in simple three variable models to estimation procedures for complex models with nonrecursive (reciprocal) linkages; we will not discuss in any detail procedures proposed by Goodman (1970, 1972, 1973) and Lehnen and Koch (1973, 1974) for the analysis of nominal and ordinal data. Chapter 2 covers Simon's (1957) work on spurious correlation and Blalock's (1964) elaboration of Simon's insight, which affords a way of testing whether linkages between variables should be included in a recursive model. In Chapter 3 attention will turn to the topics of identification and path estimation in recursive and nonrecursive models. Chapter 4 will deal with a number of special topics from a causal perspective including the consequences of random measurement error for correlation and regression coefficients and the arguments for and against treating ordinal data as interval. The chapter concludes with a general discussion of causal data analysis in the social sciences.

Before we turn to the actual analysis techniques, a number of preliminary tasks remain to be completed. The first task is to offer some comments about causal modeling as a heuristic device and not as an analysis technique. Then we must define what is meant by causality. And finally, we must lay out a set of definitions, conventions, and notation that we will use in later chapters.

## TWO USES OF CAUSAL MODELING

### Causal Theorizing and Problem Formulation

While the major concern herein will be with actual data analysis strategies, one may encounter situations in which the use of causal analysis techniques will be difficult or even impossible. For example, certain assumptions may not be met or data may be unavailable or equation systems may be unidentified. Even in such situations, a causal approach to theorizing may be valuable as a heuristic device. Thinking causally about a problem and constructing an arrow diagram that reflects causal processes may often facilitate the clearer statement of hypotheses and the generation of additional insights into the topic at hand. The heuristic value of causal thinking and arrow diagrams is demonstrated by the following example (Van Meter and Asher, 1973).

Consider the case of a decision-maker whose goal is to improve student performance on various standardized tests. Assume that the decision-maker has one basic variable over which he has control: the amount of money to be spent on education. Such a variable might be labeled a manipulable since its level can be varied by the conscious decision of actors within certain limits imposed by various external constraints. But rather than simply hypothesize that increased expenditures for education will improve student performance, one might ask the more causally relevant question: how is it that increased expenditures for education might translate into better student performance? That is, what are the ways in which increased expenditures actually *produce* improved student performance?

The decision-maker might well recognize that options are available as to how additional moneys might best be allocated to improve student performance. For example, should money be channeled into hiring more teachers so as to lower the pupil/teacher ratio, into attracting better teachers, or into improving facilities and developing (or expanding) innovative programs? What might be the optimal mix of funding for these options? We might represent the decision-maker's situation at this stage by the following diagram.

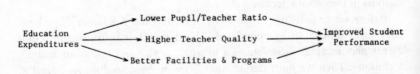

Figure 1: A Simple Arrow Diagram Indicating How Education Expenditures Might Affect Student Performance

But there are additional variables that affect student performance that are not as directly under the control of the decision-maker. These might include the supportiveness of the family environment toward educational achievement, the student's abilities, and the student's feelings toward the educational system. In addition, there might be interrelationships among the manipulable and nonmanipulable variables. For example, perhaps more and better teachers, facilities, and programs will influence the student's view of education. Hence, we might come up with the following more complete model.

Note how the model not only specifies the relationships between the independent variables and the ultimate dependent variable of interest (student performance), but also makes explicit the relationships among the prior variables. Each included linkage implicitly represents an hypothesis which would be tested by estimating the magnitude of the relationship. While actual estimation of the linkages may or may not be possible, depending upon whether satisfactory indicators can be constructed, appropriate data collected, and the like, the point to be made here is that the kind of causal thinking illustrated by the example has greater promise of increasing our understanding of social and political phenomena than simply correlating independent and dependent variables in a relatively unthinking fashion.

## CAUSAL DATA ANALYSIS

Causal data analysis is the main concern of this paper. Of course, if we are to have any confidence in the results of our analysis, then the construction of reliable and valid indicators of our key concepts is an absolute

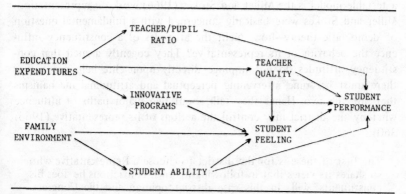

**Figure 2: A More Complex Arrow Diagram Indicating How Education Expenditures and Family Environment Might Affect Student Performance**

necessity as are appropriate data collection and data reduction strategies. While questions of reliability, validity, and the like do not directly concern us herein, the reader should clearly recognize that the success of one's data analysis depends upon proper execution of all the steps in the research process prior to the analysis stage. In fact, I would go so far as to argue that if one's causal analysis goes astray, it will more likely be due to carrying out the earlier steps in the research process poorly rather than to any misuse of the techniques which are relatively straightforward and easily learned. Poor theory, unsatisfactory operational definitions, and the like are more likely to frustrate analysis than any mistakes in application of techniques. If one errs in the actual application of techniques, the analysis can in most instances be redone correctly. But if one has omitted a key variable from the data collection or invalidly measured a key concept, then statistically "correct" analysis may still yield incorrect results.

Probably the best advice that one could offer to someone contemplating the use of causal modeling is to begin with a model in which one has substantial confidence. Presumably this confidence results from some theoretical or substantive reasoning about the linkages between the variables of interest. If one has some confidence in the basic model, then the admissible revisions in the model when the data analysis is not fully confirmatory (and it seldom is) are limited. But if one has little confidence in few, if any, of the posited linkages, then the application of causal modeling techniques may become a mindless attempt to find the best fit to the data, regardless whether the final result is substantively and theoretically plausible. One should not allow the testing and revising of models to become an enterprise completely determined by statistical results devoid of theoretical underpinnings.

An excellent example of sound prior theorizing in the construction of a testable model is the Miller and Stokes (1966) work on representation. Miller and Stokes were basically concerned with a fundamental question of democratic theory—how might the attitudes of a constituency influence the behavior of its representative? They cogently argued that constituency attitudes do not impinge directly upon elite behavior; rather there must be some intervening perceptual and attitudinal mechanisms that link the two. Hence they talk about two major paths of influence whereby the district may control the actions of its representative (1966: 360):

The first of these is for the district to choose a Representative who so shares its views that in following his own convictions he does his constituents' will. In this case district opinion and the Congressman's actions are connected through the Representative's own policy attitudes. The second means of constituency control is for the Congressman to follow his (at least tolerably accurate) perceptions of district attitude in order to win re-election. In this case constituency opinion and the Congressman's actions are connected through his perception of what the district wants.

This verbal formulation is depicted very clearly in Figure 3; note that the linkages drawn faithfully reflect their basic theory. For example, there is no direct linkage between $X_1$ and $X_4$; instead the effect of $X_1$ on $X_4$ (our basic substantive concern) is an indirect one, mediated by $X_2$ and $X_3$. Note also that two linkages were included between $X_2$ and $X_3$; this reflects the likelihood that attitudes and perceptions mutually influence each other over time. The linkage between $X_2$ and $X_3$ is commonly labelled a reciprocal or nonrecursive linkage.

## THE NOTION OF CAUSALITY

Causal modeling techniques do not allow one to determine the direction of causality between two variables nor do they allow one to conclude that a causal relationship exists, except under a restrictive set of conditions. These limitations can be explicated by examining a variety of definitions of causality. A number of writers, including Selltiz et al. (1959), specify three conditions that must be met in order to infer the existence of a causal relationship between two variables X and Y. The first condition states that there must be concomitant variation or covariation between X and Y, while the second condition requires a temporal asymmetry or time ordering between the two. These two conditions are not very troublesome for we can often measure covariation and observe or impose a temporal sequence between two variables.[1] The third condition is more problematic, requiring the elimination of other possible causal

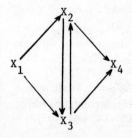

$X_1$ -- district attitudes

$X_2$ -- Representative's perceptions of constituency attitudes

$X_3$ -- Representative's attitudes

$X_4$ -- Representative's behavior

Figure 3: The Miller and Stokes Representation Model

factors that may be producing the observed relationship between X and Y. Restated, this third condition asserts that for there to be a causal relationship between X and Y, the covariation between X and Y should not vanish when the effects of confounding variables—those variables causally prior to both X and Y—are removed.

The third condition requires that we rule out all other possible causal factors. On what grounds can we make this decision with any degree of confidence? There is a potentially infinite universe of such variables and there is no statistical test or coefficient that can tell us whether we have made the correct decision. Yet at some point we must establish closure in our model and examine the relationships among a finite set of measured variables. The choice of which variables to include in the the model is a function of substantive and theoretical insights into the problem under investigation. We must try to identify confounding variables and formally incorporate (measure) them in our model. If someone is able to identify a confounding factor not included in the model, then we should actually measure such a variable and incorporate it in a revised model. But if we are simply told that confounding variables may exist without any specific clues as to their identify, we might decide to proceed forthwith to the analysis. If we are not willing at some point to proceed on an "as if" basis—as if confounding variables presented no problem—then we will be paralyzed in our efforts at data analysis.[2] As Blalock (1964: 26) argues:

> No matter how elaborate the design, certain simplifying assumptions must always be made. In particular, we must at some point assume that the effects of confounding factors are negligible. Randomization helps to rule out some of such variables, but the plausibility of this particular kind of simplifying assumption is always a question of degree.

In causal modeling, the simplifying assumptions to which Blalock alludes are generally contained in assertions about the properties of unmeasured residual or error terms.[3] Residual variables will be defined in the next section, while assumptions about such variables will be discussed in Chapter 2.

### DEFINITIONS AND NOTATION

The Miller and Stokes representation model provides a useful vehicle for laying out definitions and notational conventions. Their model is represented more completely in Figure 4 where $X_1$, $X_2$, $X_3$, and $X_4$ are as defined in Figure 3.

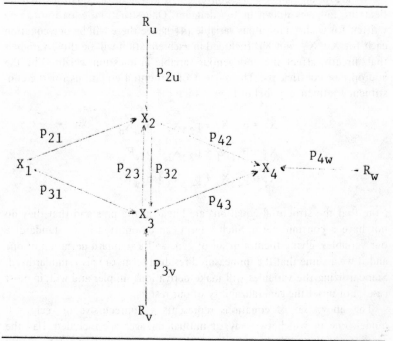

**Figure 4: The Miller and Stokes Representation Model with Residual Variables and Path Coefficients Included**

Three kinds of variables can be identified in the diagram. $X_1$ is termed an exogenous variable since it is not influenced by other variables in the model. $X_2$, $X_3$, and $X_4$ are endogenous variables which are affected by other variables in the model. The $R_i$'s are residual or error or disturbance terms that represent those factors not actually measured that impinge upon the endogenous variables. For example, $R_w$ might include the effects of such variables as the preferences of the president and the party leadership—both of which might influence the legislator's behavior, but neither of which is formally measured in the model. If we thought that the president's position also impinged upon the representative's attitudes, then presidential position would be a confounding variable and we would want to expand our model to include it as a fifth variable with linkages to $X_3$ and $X_4$.

In general, we can say that the $X_i$'s are measured variables—variables for which data have been collected—while the $R_i$'s are unmeasured variables for which observation have not been gathered. For now, we will refer to the $p_{ij}$'s as unknown weights that represent the impact of one variable upon another. Later we will label these weights path coefficients.

An arrow diagram can be converted to a system of equations that reflect the linkages drawn in the diagram. One structural equation can be written for each endogenous variable;[4] hence there will be one equation each for $X_2$, $X_3$, and $X_4$. Included in each equation will be those variables that directly affect the endogenous variable in question weighted by the appropriate coefficients. The system of structural equations for the constituency influence model of Figure 4 is:

$$X_2 = p_{21}X_1 + p_{23}X_3 + p_{2u}R_u$$
$$X_3 = p_{31}X_1 + p_{32}X_2 + p_{3v}R_v$$
$$X_4 = p_{42}X_2 + p_{43}X_3 + p_{4w}R_w$$

Note that the structural equations are linear in the $p_{ij}$'s and that they do not have a constant term. Such a term can be omitted if we standardize our variables, giving them a mean of zero and a standard deviation of one and if we assume that the unmeasured residual terms are also standardized. Standardizing the variables will make derivations simpler and will, in most cases, not upset the generalizability of our results.

The above set of equations represents a nonrecursive or reciprocal model, one in which two-way or mutual linkages are included. Had the arrow from $X_3$ to $X_2$ been omitted, the structural equation for $X_2$ would have been

$$X_2 = p_{21}X_1 + p_{2u}R_u$$

and we would have a recursive system of equations. Verbally, recursiveness implies that there are no feedback loops or reciprocal linkages. Mathematically, we know that if in a recursive system $p_{ij} \neq 0$, then $p_{ji} = 0$.[5]

While additional definitions and notation will be introduced later, the ones presented provide sufficient background to analyze the work of Herbert Simon. The reader unfamiliar with mathematical expectation and properties of standardized variables is advised to look at Appendix A before proceeding.

## 2. THE WORK OF SIMON AND BLALOCK

### OVERVIEW

Much of the work that employs causal modeling techniques takes advantage of Simon's insight into the problem of spurious correlation and

Blalock's extension of Simon's insight into an arrow testing procedure for multivariate models. The work of Simon is particularly interesting in that it is directly linked to developments in causal analysis in sociology, as exemplified by the Simon-Blalock technique, and to developments in econometrics, as evidenced by the path estimation that Simon *implicitly* performs. In this chapter, we will first lay out the work of Simon and simultaneously introduce a procedure for estimating the magnitude of path coefficients. Then attention will turn to the work of Blalock, focusing on the assumptions of the Simon-Blalock technique, the relaxation of these assumptions, and a cost-benefits analysis of the Simon-Blalock technique.

### SIMON AND SPURIOUS CORRELATION

Simon is basically interested in the conditions under which a nonzero correlation between two variables provides evidence for inferring the existence of a causal relationship between the two. Simon analyzes the bivariate situation first, asserting (1957: 42-43): "correlation is a proof of causation in the two variable case if we are willing to make the assumptions of time precedence and noncorrelation of the error terms." The situation that Simon is discussing is represented by the arrow diagram and structural equations in Figure 5; the notation corresponds to that presented in the first chapter and not to Simon's.

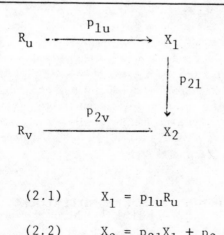

$$(2.1) \quad X_1 = p_{1u}R_u$$

$$(2.2) \quad X_2 = p_{21}X_1 + p_{2v}R_v$$

**Figure 5: The Simon Two Variable Model and Structural Equations**

What Simon's assumptions require is that if there be a causal relationship between $X_1$ and $X_2$, we are able to specify a priori what the direction of that relationship is. Note that in Figure 5, $X_1$ influences $X_2$ and not the reverse; the coefficient $p_{21}$ represents the causal impact of $X_1$ on $X_2$. The other assumption requires that the residuals associated with $X_1$ and $X_2$ be uncorrelated, that is, that $R_u$ and $R_v$ are uncorrelated. The uncorrelated residuals assumption is basically equivalent to the assertion that there is no confounding variable impinging upon both $X_1$ and $X_2$ where by a confounding variable is meant any unmeasured factor that directly influences two or more of the measured variables. Given these assumptions, Simon finds that the estimate of $p_{21}$ is simply the correlation between $X_1$ and $X_2-r_{12}$.

This result means that correlation is evidence of causation under the set of assumptions made. One should realize, however, that the assumptions are quite stringent, particularly the second assumption about uncorrelated residuals. How can we be fully confident that there are no confounding variables? The answer is that we cannot, but we must proceed on an "as if" basis.

Simon's analysis then moves to a three variable situation in which the basic concern is whether the observed correlation between two variables is spurious—due to the presence of a third variable impinging upon both— or whether the observed correlation indicates any causal relationship between the two variables in question. This three variable situation is shown in the diagram and structural equations of Figure 6; from now on, no

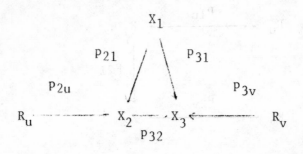

$$(2.3) \qquad X_2 = p_{21}X_1 + p_{2u}R_u$$

$$(2.4) \qquad X_3 = p_{31}X_1 + p_{32}X_2 + p_{3v}R_v$$

Figure 6: The Simon Three Variable Model and Structural Equations

equation will be included for the exogenous variable (in this case $X_1$) for reasons detailed in note 4.

Assume that there is a nonvanishing zero order correlation between $X_2$ and $X_3$. We want to know whether $p_{32}$ is also nonzero; if it is, this means that $X_2$ has a causal impact on $X_3$. Thus, Simon is concerned with the conditions under which $p_{32}$ vanishes. He employs a cumbersome procedure of multiplying pairs of equations together to come up with an estimate for $p_{32}$ and then examines this estimate to determine when it would take on the value of zero.

An easier way of obtaining an estimate for $p_{32}$ is to operate on equation 2.4 by means of an instrumental variable procedure. The instrumental variable procedure involves operating on each structural equation so as to yield a system of m equations in n unknowns (the $p_{ij}$'s) where $m \geqslant n$. Appropriate instrumental variables for operating on a specific structural equation are those variables uncorrelated with the residual term in that structural equation. In Chapter 3 we discuss in greater detail instrumental variable estimation procedures and desirable properties of variables that make them useful as instruments.

For the three variable model under consideration, we are assuming that the residual variables are pairwise uncorrelated. We are also assuming that the explanatory variables in any structural equation are uncorrelated with the residual variable in that equation. For example, we assume in equation 2.3 that $X_1$ and $R_u$ are uncorrelated and in equation 2.4 that $X_1$ and $X_2$ are both uncorrelated with $R_v$. These assumptions are not testable by statistical methods; rather we must convince ourselves of their validity on substantive grounds. These assumptions will be discussed further in the context of the basic regression model later.

Since a variable must be uncorrelated with the residual term in the equation in which it is being used as an instrument, note that $X_1$ and $X_2$ can serve as instruments for equation 2.4; $X_3$ is not an appropriate instrument for this equation since $X_3$ and $R_v$ are clearly correlated as indicated by the linkage drawn between them. The instrumental variable procedure is described in Stokes (1974); basically it entails multiplying equations by instruments, taking expected values, simplifying and solving. To solve for $p_{32}$ (and $p_{31}$) we would multiply equation 2.4 by $X_1$, take the expected value, and simplify, and repeat the same steps with $X_2$ as the instrument. This would yield two equations in the two unknowns $p_{31}$ and $p_{32}$. The actual calculations are shown in Appendix B.

The solution for $p_{32}$ using either Simon's method or the instrumental variable procedure is

$$p_{32} = \frac{r_{23} - r_{12}r_{13}}{1 - r_{12}^2}$$

This solution in effect is a precise estimate of $p_{32}$; however, Simon is interested in the case where $p_{32}$ vanishes and he observes that the coefficient will vanish when its numerator goes to zero. Hence, Simon focuses on the numerator of the expression and we no longer have an estimate for $p_{32}$. The important feature of Simon's solution for $p_{32}$ is that it is equivalent to the standardized regression coefficient (beta weight) $B_{32 \cdot 1}$. That is,

$$p_{32} = B_{32 \cdot 1} = \frac{r_{23} - r_{12}r_{13}}{1 - r_{12}^2}$$

It is also important to note in general that the numerator of a standardized regression coefficient is the same as the numerator of the corresponding partial correlation coefficient. Hence, Simon observes that the numerator of $p_{32}$ is equal to the numerator of the partial correlation coefficient $r_{23 \cdot 1}$. Thus, if the beta goes to zero, so must the corresponding partial r since they have the same numerator. Hence, Simon presents predictions about the vanishing of certain partial correlation coefficients to test whether a correlation is spurious. But these predictions rest upon an underlying regression justification, a crucial consideration for our later discussion of the Simon-Blalock technique.

Simon (1957: 43-48) and Alker (1965: 116-126) develop correlational predictions for other three variable models. For example, if the developmental sequence $X_1 \rightarrow X_2 \rightarrow X_3$ is the correct model linking the three variables, then one would predict that $r_{13} = r_{12}r_{23}$ or equivalently that $r_{13 \cdot 2} = 0$. A substantive example may be helpful here. The interrelationships among levels of socioeconomic development, characteristics of political systems, and policy outputs have been the focus of considerable research by students of American state politics. Early work (Key, 1949; Lockard, 1959) talked about the impact of the party system on policy outputs; states characterized by more competitive party systems were found to be more "liberal" in their welfare policy outputs. Dawson and Robinson (1963) formulated a three variable developmental model in which interparty competition intervened between the socioeconomic development of a state and its policy outputs. Their findings pointed to the possibility of a spurious relationship in which the correlation between party competition and policy outputs vanished when the effects of socioeconomic development were controlled. These basic alternatives are shown

[19]

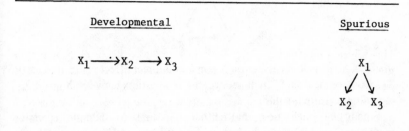

predictions: $r_{13.2} = 0$                              $r_{23.1} = 0$

**Figure 7: Developmental and Spurious Models of the Interrelationships Among Socioeconomic Development, Interparty Competition, and Welfare Policy Outputs**

in Figure 7 where $X_1$ is the level of socioeconomic development of a state, $X_2$ the level of interparty competition, and $X_3$ the extent of welfare benefits. If we have collected observations on the three variables, we can generate predictions to allow us to determine whether the spurious or developmental model is more appropriate.

Blalock notes that the use of regression coefficients to distinguish between the two models will yield more precise predictions as indicated in Table 1. In all cases the regression coefficients give specific predictions, while the correlation coefficients yield imprecise predictions in two cases. Blalock's advocacy of regression coefficients is certainly well argued, although it should be noted that his suggestions are most useful when one has a pure spurious or pure developmental model. In most practical data analysis situations, one will likely have relationships that are part spurious and part developmental. This is, the relationships will look like

**TABLE 1**
**A Comparison of Regression and Correlation Predictions for Spurious and Developmental Models**

| Developmental | | Spurious | |
|---|---|---|---|
| Correlation | Regression | Correlation | Regression |
| $r_{13.2} = 0$ | $B_{31.2} = 0$ | $r_{13.2} = ?$ | $B_{31.2} = B_{31} = r_{13}$ |
| $r_{23.1} < r_{23}$ | $B_{32.1} = B_{32} = r_{23}$ | $r_{23.1} = 0$ | $B_{32.1} = 0$ |

where $X_1$ has a direct effect on $X_3$ and an indirect effect via its impact on $X_2$. Controlling for $X_1$ will reduce the correlation between $X_2$ and $X_3$, but will not make it vanish.

Finally, we might note that neither the correlation nor the regression predictions enable us to distinguish between the following two models. For example, in both cases we would predict that $r_{23 \cdot 1} = 0$.

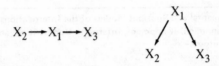

In order to choose between the two configurations, we must add some substantive information about the causal ordering among the variables. Does $X_1$ influence $X_2$ or the reverse? This is a question that the statistics cannot answer; instead, the answer must emerge from some theoretical or substantive insights about the problem at hand.

### THE SIMON-BLALOCK TECHNIQUE

### The Basic Technique

Blalock took Simon's work on three variable models and expanded it into a technique that allows one to test for the existence of linkages between variables in recursive models of any size. Blalock's technique, while yielding only limited information, is still fairly popular in the social sciences despite Blalock's advocacy of more sophisticated and powerful estimation procedures. The results of the technique tell us simply whether or not a linkage should be included in a model; if the decision is made to incorporate the linkage, little has been said about its magnitude except that it meets some minimum level required for inclusion.

The basic steps in the Simon-Blalock technique are to construct a model, often in the form of an arrow diagram, observe where linkages between pairs of variables have been omitted, and generate predictions that certain partial correlation coefficients involving those pairs of variables should go to zero. One then calculates the actual value of the partial correlation, compares it to the predicted value, and on the basis of the comparison makes a decision about whether a linkage is to be omitted or not.

As in Simon's work, the use of predictions in the form of partial correlation coefficients is based upon an underlying regression rationale as will be demonstrated below. Consider the four variable model and set of structural equations in Figure 8. Note that we have a recursive system. If we again assume that the residual variables are pairwise uncorrelated and are uncorrelated with the explanatory variables in the equations with which they appear, then the $p_{ij}$'s can be estimated by ordinary least squares procedures and in fact are standardized regression coefficients when our variables are in standard form. Thus, the structural equations can be rewritten as:

$$X_2 = B_{21}X_1 + p_{2u}R_u \qquad [2.8]$$

$$X_3 = B_{31 \cdot 2}X_1 + B_{32 \cdot 1}X_2 + p_{3v}R_v \qquad [2.9]$$

$$X_4 = B_{41 \cdot 23}X_1 + B_{42 \cdot 13}X_2 + B_{43 \cdot 12}X_3 + p_{4w}R_w \qquad [2.10]$$

Hence, whenever a linkage has been omitted from a recursive model, a certain regression coefficient has been set equal to zero. But since the beta and the corresponding partial correlation coefficient share the same numerator, setting a regression coefficient to zero is equivalent to predicting

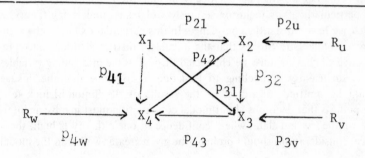

$$(2.5) \qquad X_2 = p_{21}X_1 + p_{2u}R_u$$

$$(2.6) \qquad X_3 = p_{31}X_1 + p_{32}X_2 + p_{3v}R_v$$

$$(2.7) \qquad X_4 = p_{41}X_1 + p_{42}X_2 + p_{43}X_3 + p_{4w}R_w$$

Figure 8: A Four Variable Recursive Model and Structural Equations

that the corresponding partial r should also be equal to zero. For example, if in our four variable model the linkage between $X_2$ and $X_4$ had been omitted, then $p_{42}$ would have been set equal to zero which means that $B_{42 \cdot 13}$ is posited to be vanishing. But if $B_{42 \cdot 13}$ is zero, then the corresponding partial correlation $r_{24 \cdot 13}$ should also be zero. Thus, an examination of the appropriate partial correlation becomes a test of whether a linkage should be included or excluded from a model.

In short, in using the Simon-Blalock technique, one looks for pairs of variables between which linkages have been omitted and generates predictions that the correlations between those pairs of variables controlling for appropriate other variables should be zero. According to Blalock, one controls for all those variables prior to or intervening between the two variables in question. For example, in the Miller and Stokes representation model depicted in Figure 3 of Chapter 1 (without the linkage from $X_3$ to $X_2$), a linkage was omitted between district attitudes ($X_1$) and representative's behavior ($X_4$). One would predict here that $r_{14 \cdot 23}$ equals zero. One would then compute the actual value of the partial r, compare it to the predicted value, and make a decision about including the linkage or not. It turns out in this example that the calculated partial r is sufficiently close to zero so the decision is to omit the linkage. For the sake of argument, however, let us assume that the partial r was significantly different from zero. Do we than automatically include the linkage? The answer is no, particularly if its inclusion seriously violates an underlying theory in which we have substantial confidence. In this particular example, the argument of Miller and Stokes that the impact of district attitudes on representative's behavior must be channeled through some intervening variables seems sufficiently compelling to lead one to conclude that the linkage should be omitted, regardless of the results of the Simon-Blalock test. The point is that decisions about model construction must involve an interplay of theory and data; where confidence in one's theory is high, theoretical considerations should probably be given greater weight in the model testing.

Another example of the Simon-Blalock technique is provided by the Goldberg (1966) work on voting behavior. The first model analyzed by Goldberg is presented in Figure 9 along with the Simon-Blalock predictions for the model. Note that many of the predictions in Goldberg's first model do not hold—which suggests that the model is in need of revision, generally by adding linkages, dropping others, and retesting each subsequent model, a procedure carefully followed by Goldberg.

Blalock (1964: 80) suggests two general strategies of model revision:

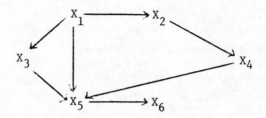

$X_1$ - father's sociological characteristics

$X_2$ - father's party identification

$X_3$ - respondent's sociological characteristics

$X_4$ - respondent's party identification

$X_5$ - respondent's partisan attitudes

$X_6$ - respondent's vote

| Prediction equations | Actual values |
|---|---|
| $r_{41 \cdot 23} = 0$ | 0.017 |
| $r_{61 \cdot 2345} = 0$ | -0.019 |
| $r_{32 \cdot 1} = 0$ | 0.101 |
| $r_{52 \cdot 134} = 0$ | 0.032 |
| $r_{62 \cdot 1345} = 0$ | 0.053 |
| $r_{43 \cdot 12} = 0$ | 0.130 |
| $r_{63 \cdot 1245} = 0$ | -0.022 |
| $r_{64 \cdot 1235} = 0$ | 0.365 |

Figure 9: The First Goldberg Model with Simon-Blalock Predictions and Actual Values

(1) make revisions early in the model so that the effects of these revisions will be transmitted throughout the system of relationships, and

(2) revise where the discrepancies are greatest between the predicted and actual values.

As suggested above, a third strategy might be to make revisions where one has the greatest substantive justification for so doing. It is important to note that in revising a model, what is in question is whether a linkage between two variables is warranted; what is not in question is the direction of that linkage. That is, one must specify the causal ordering among the variables a priori; the Simon-Blalock technique does not provide a test for the direction of causality. See the work of Forbes and Tufte (1968) for an elaboration of this point.

There are a number of problems associated with the Simon-Blalock technique. One relatively minor one concerns how large the difference between actual and predicted partial r's must be to conclude that the predictions do not hold. It is not uncommon for investigators to employ arbitrary decision rules such as: differences greater than .05 (or .1) suggest the need for model revisions, while differences less than .05 (or .1) confirm the model as is.

A more serious problem with the Simon-Blalock technique is that mindless model revision is likely to lead to a final model with no linkages omitted. Hence there will be no predictions or tests of the model. For each linkage that is omitted, a prediction is generated that serves as a test of the adequacy of the model. These predictions may be thought of as excess equations in an equation system; each omitted linkage yields one element of overdetermination. That is, each linkage excluded from a model reduces the number of unknowns by one, resulting in an equation system with more equations than unknowns. This situation raises the possibility of multiple and divergent solutions for the unknowns, a point discussed extensively in Chapter 3.

## Assumptions of the Simon-Blalock Technique

Since the justification for the Simon-Blalock technique rests in the basic regression model, the proper use of the technique requires satisfaction of the assumptions of regression analysis. Thus, we will now explicate these assumptions and discuss briefly how each might be relaxed. First, however, we will discuss the general linear statistical (regression) model using notation that corresponds to that commonly found in mathematics texts.

The general linear model relates a dependent variable Y to a set of independent or predictor or explanatory variables $X_1, X_2 \ldots, X_k$ in the following fashion.

$$Y = b_0 + b_1 X_1 + b_2 X_2 + \ldots + b_k X_k + e$$

The $b_i$'s are unknown parameters that measure the respective weights assigned to each of the independent variables in the prediction of Y. e is an error term that arises from two sources:

(1) a stochastic error component (Wonnacott and Wonnacott, 1970: 17; Deegan, 1972: 7) resulting from the effects on Y of many omitted variables operating in different directions and each with a relatively small effect, and

(2) a measurement error component.

A number of assumptions are made about the general linear model and estimation based upon it. Deegan classifies these assumptions into three categories, those "necessary for certain mathematical operations such as determining means and variances, those assumptions needed for least squares operations, and those assumptions relied on for significance testing." In the first category, we require interval level data to justify the use of the Pearson product-moment correlations employed in the Simon-Blalock technique. The second class of assumptions is those needed for estimation; these focus on assumptions about the error term. We make four basic assumptions about the error term:

(1) its mean is zero;

(2) it has a constant variance for different values of an $X_i$ (homoscedasticity);

(3) pairs of error terms are uncorrelated; and

(4) the independent variables and error term in the same equation are uncorrelated.

Violation of this last assumption leads to estimates with undesirable properties, a topic developed later. The last set of assumptions deals with the applicability of significance tests; if we want to employ such tests, we must assume that the error term is normally distributed.

The general linear model entails additional restrictions, one being the structure of the relationships is linear in the $b_i$'s. Furthermore, it is assumed that the independent variables are measured without error. If the independent variables do contain random measurement error (to be defined later), then the obtained partial r's and partial betas will be attenuated (reduced), a situation more worrisome in the multivariate case since certain coefficients may be biased more than others, thereby creating difficulties in making inferences about the relative effects of the independent variables. Random measurement error in the dependent variable, however, will attenuate only the correlation coefficients and not the regression coefficients. If the measurement error is nonrandom or systematic, then the obtained coefficients may be biased either upward or downward.

Thus, the Simon-Blalock technique requires one to make a large number of stringent, unrealistic assumptions. One must assume that the data are interval in order to properly calculate correlation coefficients. Monte Carlo (computer simulation) techniques can be used to determine the consequences of violating this assumption. There are arguments for and against treating ordinal data as interval which will be considered in Chapter 4. Thus, the interval level assumption does not appear to be a troublesome one.

The Simon-Blalock technique also requires a recursive system since in a nonrecursive system, one of the crucial assumptions about the behavior of the residual variables is patently false. An examination of the nonrecursive version of the Miller and Stokes model in Figure 4 illustrates this point; the structural equations for the model are:

$$X_2 = p_{21}X_1 + p_{23}X_3 + p_{2u}R_u \qquad [2.11]$$

$$X_3 = p_{31}X_1 + p_{32}X_2 + p_{3v}R_v \qquad [2.12]$$

$$X_4 = p_{42}X_2 + p_{43}X_3 + p_{4w}R_w \qquad [2.13]$$

To correctly apply ordinary regression procedures to equation 2.11, one would have to assume that $R_u$ is uncorrelated with $X_1$ and $X_3$. But this cannot be the case since $R_u$ influences $X_2$ which influences $X_3$; therefore $R_u$ and $X_3$ will be correlated. Likewise, ordinary regression analysis is inappropriate for equation 2.12 since $R_v$ and $X_2$ are correlated. Hence, the inclusion of the reciprocal linkage makes our error assumptions, which were unrealistic in the recursive case, even more absurd in the nonrecursive situation.

It has been suggested that one way to handle feedback loops and reciprocal linkages within the context of a recursive model is to lag our variables, to collect observations on our variables at repeated points in time. Thus, instead of having $X \rightleftharpoons Y$, we might instead have $X_{t-1} \rightarrow Y_t \rightarrow X_{t+1}$. However, this procedure is easier said than done for a number of reasons.

Even if one has the resources to collect over time data, it is still difficult to know the proper time intervals or lags at which to collect the data. While economists may have solid reasons for choosing their lags—seasons, quarters, fiscal years, and the like—most social scientists would be hard pressed to specify the appropriate lags a priori.

Another problem with lagged variables in a recursive model is that one must still assume that the residual variables are uncorrelated and this seems unlikely when one has measures of the same variables at multiple time points. This is, one would expect that the residual variables associated with the same variable measured over time would themselves be correlated. This is termed the problem of serial or autocorrelation. While there are alternative techniques to ordinary least squares in the presence of auto-correlation, these techniques get rather complicated. See Hibbs (1974) for an extensive discussion of the problem. Thus, the suggestion that the use of lagged variables enables one to remain within a recursive system is not as helpful as it first appears.

The Simon-Blalock technique also requires that our independent variables be measured without error, obviously a very unrealistic assumption given the state of much social science measurement. Of course, this unrealistic assumption is violated regularly by users of ordinary regression techniques. The problem of measurement error and some causal approaches to the problem will be considered in Chapter 4.

The Simon-Blalock technique further requires linear relationships where the linearity refers to the parameters (the b coefficients). An example of a nonlinear model is

$$Y = K X_1^{b_1} X_2^{b_2} e \qquad [2.14]$$

Before the b's in this equation can be estimated by ordinary least squares, the equation must be transformed to a linear structure. Fortunately, a transformation is available that accomplishes this; if one takes the log of both sides of equation 2.14, one obtains

$$\log Y = \log K + b_1 \log X_1 + b_2 \log X_2 + \log e \qquad [2.15]$$

Now ordinary least squares can be applied. This log transformation is used rather widely. It has been applied to the Cobb-Douglas production function to make it amenable to ordinary least squares (Wonnacott and Wonnacott, 1970: 91-98). Strouse and Williams (1972) have employed it to investigate the impact of political and economic variables on a series of policy-related dependent variables.

There is little reason to believe that the world behaves in a linear, additive fashion. The imposition of linearity on many of the phenomena we are studying seems to be more a matter of convenience rather than a well justified claim. Of course, one might argue that linearity is to be preferred to nonlinearity on the grounds of parsimony, especially when there is no theoretical reason for choosing one over the other. Where we do have reasons to opt for nonlinearity we may confront nonlinear relationships that are not as tractable by simple transformations as the example given above. In such cases, ordinary least squares will be useless and brute force, iterative (successive approximations) methods of solution may have to be utilized.

There is another meaning of linearity which is relevant to our discussion of the Simon-Blalock technique and the use of the product-moment correlation. The Pearson r measures the degree of linear relationship between two variables and one should first verify that the two variables are indeed linearly related before computing r's. (This verification could be done by visual inspection of scatterplots.) It is possible for two variables X and Y to be perfectly functionally related, yet have an intercorrelation of zero. For example, if X and Y are related by the equation $X = Y^2$, the correlation between the X and Y values will be zero.

An additional requirement of regression analysis and the Simon-Blalock technique which we have not yet discussed is that there be no specification errors. By specification error is meant an improper delineation of the causal structure among a set of variables; for example, variables that should have been included may have been left out or vice versa. Deegan (1972) and Uslaner (1976) detail the types and consequences of specification errors. For our purposes, we might simply observe that specification errors may lead to severely biased estimates which can lead to incorrect causal inferences. Bohrnstedt and Carter (1971: 141) conclude with respect to specification error that "if we hypothesize the wrong model, then our estimation of that model will yield meaningless estimates." Their conclusion is a bit exaggerated in that specification errors are more worrisome the more serious the error that has been made. That is, omitting a variable with strong effects is worse than omitting one with weak effects. Hopefully, our theories will be sufficiently developed to enable us to identify the most important variables that merit investigation, thereby minimizing the consequences of our specification errors.

The reader may be demoralized at this stage by the assumptions required for regression analysis and the Simon-Blalock technique so perhaps the conclusions of Bohrnstedt and Carter (1971: 142) should be cited here to indicate that the situation is not as dismal as it appears:

We feel there is ample evidence to suggest that regression analysis is adequately robust except in the presence of measurement and specification error. It has been shown that the problems of heteroscedasticity and nonnormality do not, in fact, generally cause serious distortions. In cases where they do, on the other hand, adequate correction procedures exist to minimize these distortions.

## Cost-Benefits Analysis of the Simon-Blalock Technique

It is now clear that proper use of the Simon-Blalock technique requires a major investment in some highly implausible assumptions. For this sizable investment, we receive a very meager return—information about whether a linkage should be included or not, with little information about the strength of that linkage if it is included. This latter information can be readily obtained by moving to estimation techniques—path analysis. Once we have estimated the linkages, we can then delineate the causal relationships underlying the observed patterns of correlations. Thus our attention in Chapter 3 turns first to recursive path analysis which requires us to make the same assumptions as the Simon-Blalock technique, but yields us much richer information.

# 3. RECURSIVE AND NONRECURSIVE PATH ESTIMATION

## RECURSIVE PATH ANALYSIS

## Obtaining the Path Estimates

Path analysis is basically concerned with estimating the magnitude of the linkages between variables and using these estimates to provide information about the underlying causal processes. The estimates can be obtained by a variety of procedures including the instrumental variable method mentioned earlier. The simplest way to obtain the path coefficients is to employ ordinary regression techniques, providing the regression assumptions are met, particularly the requirement that the residual variable in a structural equation be uncorrelated with the explanatory variables in that equation. For example, consider the recursive version of the Miller and Stokes representation model and the accompanying structural equations shown in Figure 10.

To obtain estimates of the main path coefficients, one simply regresses each endogenous variable on those variables that directly impinge upon it. $p_{21}$ would be gotten by regressing $X_2$ on $X_1$, $p_{31}$ and $p_{32}$ obtained by

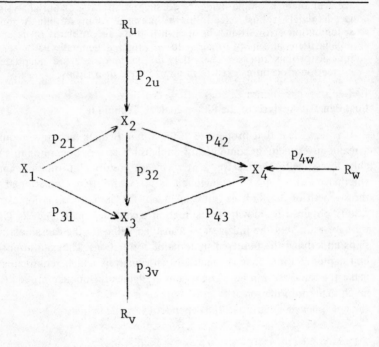

(3.1)  $X_2 = p_{21}X_1 + p_{2u}R_u$

(3.2)  $X_3 = p_{31}X_1 + p_{32}X_2 + p_{3v}R_v$

(3.3)  $X_4 = p_{42}X_2 + p_{43}X_3 + p_{4w}R_w$

$X_1$ — district attitudes

$X_2$ — representative's perceptions of
        constituency attitudes

$X_3$ — representative's attitudes

$X_4$ — representative's behavior

Figure 10:  The Recursive Version of the Miller and Stokes Model

regressing $X_3$ on $X_1$ and $X_2$, and $p_{42}$ and $p_{43}$ determined by regressing $X_4$ on $X_2$ and $X_3$. Note that in calculating $p_{42}$ and $p_{43}$, $X_1$ does not serve as a predictor of $X_4$ because it does not have a direct effect on $X_4$. The residual path coefficients can also be ascertained by ordinary regression analysis since they have a direct regression interpretation. The general form of a residual path coefficient is $\sqrt{1 - R^2}$ where $R^2$ is the square of the appropriate multiple correlation coefficient. In the representation model of Figure 10,

$$p_{2u} = \sqrt{1 - r_{12}^2}$$

$$p_{3v} = \sqrt{1 - R_{3 \cdot 12}^2}$$

$$p_{4w} = \sqrt{1 - R_{4 \cdot 23}^2}$$

Note that the $R^2$ is commonly referred to as the fraction or proportion of explained variance. Since standardized variables have a variance of one, the general expression $1 - R^2$ is simply the proportion of unexplained variance. Therefore, the residual path coefficient is simply the square root of the unexplained variation in the dependent variable in question.

Stokes (1974) has provided a demonstration of the equivalence of the regression and the instrumental variable results. Basically, the instrumental variable procedure involves operating on the structural equations with variables called instruments, the key property of instrumental variables being that they are uncorrelated with the residual terms in the equations in which they are used. In general, given a recursive system and the necessary assumptions about residual terms, the instrumental variable technique yields at least as many equations as unknowns so that one can always get a solution for the path coefficients, assuming the equations are linearly independent.[6] In fact, except for models in which every possible linkage that maintains the recursiveness of the system has been included, the instrumental variable method will generate more equations than unknowns. The problem then becomes choosing a subset of equations to obtain estimates of the unknown path coefficients. It is likely that different subsets of equations will yield different solutions, certainly an unsatisfactory state of affairs. The excess equations—those not used in obtaining a solution—can be used to test the model. That is, the results derived from one subset of equations can be substituted into the unused equations and, if there is consistency, we would have additional confidence in the soundness of our model. But often inconsistencies arise and the choice of which solution to keep remains. This is basically a problem of overidentification, a topic to be considered later. For now, we might simply state that where there are excess instruments available, the use of only those instruments that also appear in the structural equation under scrutiny will generate estimates that are ordinary regression coefficients. For example, in equation 3.3, only two instrumental variables are needed to solve for $p_{42}$ and $p_{43}$. Yet there are three variables—$X_1$, $X_2$, and $X_3$—that can legitimately serve as instruments (Stokes, 1974: 203-204). The use of all three variables will generate a system of three equations in two unknowns, and picking subsets of equations to solve for $p_{42}$ and $p_{43}$ is likely to lead to estimates that are somewhat inconsistent. If one wants his estimates to be regression coefficients (reasons why one might desire this will be given later), one should use as the instruments $X_2$ and $X_3$ since they also appear in the structural equation for $X_4$.

In summary, recursive path analysis can be carried out within the context of ordinary regression analysis and does not require the learning of any new analysis techniques with the proviso that the issue is still open as to how to optimally treat the situation of excess equations. The real utility of path analysis comes in what one does with the path estimates once they are determined.

## Advantages of Path Analysis

One of the main advantages of path analysis is that it enables one to measure the direct and indirect effects that one variable has upon another. In our earlier public policy example, socioeconomic development has a direct effect on policy outputs and also an indirect effect via its impact on interparty competition. Similarly, in the Miller and Stokes example, constituency attitudes have an indirect effect on the representative's behavior via their impact on the representative's attitudes and his perceptions of the constituency's attitudes. One could then compare the magnitude of the direct and indirect effects which would identify the operative causal mechanisms.

In addition, path analysis enables us to decompose the correlation between any two variables into a sum of simple and compound paths with some of these compound paths being substantively meaningful indirect effects and others perhaps not. The importance of this latter distinction will be clarified later. The decomposition of the correlation can be done in a number of ways. One way is to operate on the reduced form of the structural equations; reduced form equations are ones in which the dependent variable is expressed in terms of exogenous variables only. Stokes (1974: 206-208) presents an example of this potentially tedious procedure. An equivalent procedure is to utilize the following expression:

$$r_{ij} = \sum_k p_{ik} r_{jk}$$

where k is an index referencing those variables having a direct impact on $X_i$ and the subscript i references the dependent variable in the pair.

Unfortunately, this equation is also tedious to use in decomposing correlations.[7] Fortunately, there is a third method available and that is simply to read the simple and compound paths directly from the arrow diagram using some rules attributable to Sewall Wright (1934). Wright's rules consist of two definitions and three instructions as to how a correlation is actually decomposed. The definitions are simply that any correlation between two variables can be decomposed into a sum of simple and compound paths, and that a compound path is equal to the product of the simple paths comprising it. The three instructions are:

(a) no path may pass through the same variable more than once;
(b) no path may go backward on (against the direction of) an arrow after the path has gone forward on a different arrow;
(c) no path may pass through a double-headed curved arrow (representing an unanalyzed correlation between exogenous variables) more than once in any single path.

The easiest way of applying Wright's rules is to imagine that one is trying to move from one variable to another in a causal diagram without violating any of Wright's instructions. For example, in the Miller and Stokes model, we can decompose the correlation between $X_1$ and $X_3$ by imagining we are trying to go from $X_1$ to $X_3$ while obeying Wright's rules. We could go directly from $X_1$ to $X_3$ and this would be represented by the simple path $p_{31}$. We also could go from $X_1$ to $X_2$ to $X_3$, a compound path represented by the product $p_{21}p_{32}$. These are the only ways of going from $X_1$ to $X_3$; thus the decomposition of $r_{13}$ is the sum of the simple and compound paths or $p_{31} + p_{21}p_{32}$. $p_{31}$ is commonly termed the direct effect of $X_1$ on $X_3$, while the compound path $p_{21}p_{32}$ is a substantively interpretable indirect effect of $X_1$ on $X_3$. As another example, consider the decomposition of the correlation $r_{23}$. Again we ask how can we go from $X_2$ to $X_3$ without violating any of Wright's rules. We can clearly go directly from $X_2$ to $X_3$—$p_{32}$—and we can go from $X_2$ to $X_1$ to $X_3$—$p_{21}p_{31}$. This compound path does not violate rule (b) since the path goes backward and then forward on an arrow and not the reverse. Thus the decomposition of $r_{23}$ equals $p_{32} + p_{21}p_{31}$. This latter compound path is *not* a substantively meaningful indirect effect since it violates the causal ordering among the variables; it is however a legitimate part of the correlation decomposition. The path $p_{21}p_{31}$ is included in the decomposition of $r_{23}$ since a part of the correlation between $X_2$ and $X_3$ is due to the common impact of $X_1$ on both variables. Thus, all indirect effects are compound paths, but not all compound paths are substantively interpretable indirect effects. This is an important point to note since there is much confusion in the literature; some people have defined the indirect effects to be equal to the correlation minus the direct effect. This can be incorrect since it would include among the indirect effects those compound paths that cannot be meaningfully considered indirect effects. Hence, we might talk of decomposing correlations into three components: direct effects, indirect effects, and spurious effects, the latter referring to those compound paths that are mathematically part of the decomposition, but are not substantively interpretable. The complete decomposition of the correlations in the Miller and Stokes model are given in Appendix C for those readers who want to check their comprehension of Wright's rules; also presented is an illustration of the violation of the first of Wright's rules.

The decomposition of the correlation is extremely important since it yields information about the causal processes as will be illustrated in an example to be presented shortly. The decomposition also provides a way in which to test the adequacy of the model if some linkages have initially been omitted. If the model were specified correctly, then (except for measurement error and sampling error when relevant) the empirical correlation between any two variables should be numerically equal to the sum of the simple and compound paths linking the two variables. If the equality does not hold, this suggests that the model may be improperly specified and in need of revision. This procedure is entirely analogous to the Simon-Blalock technique; if no linkages have been omitted in the model, the correlation decomposition cannot serve as a test of the model since the relationship between the empirical correlation and the sum of the simple and compound paths in such a situation is one of a mathematical identity.

Using correlation decomposition as a test of the model may entail substantial work; fortunately a much simpler procedure is available. If a linkage has been omitted from the model, implicitly we have said that we expect the magnitude of the path coefficient to be zero. Thus, the test of the model becomes whether the omitted coefficient is indeed zero, the magnitude of the omitted linkage being determined by estimating the model with the linkage under question included.

In summary, recursive path analysis tells us everything that the Simon-Blalock technique tells us plus a lot more, and all for the same investment in assumptions. Path analysis is also superior to ordinary regression analysis since it allows us to move beyond the estimation of direct effects, the basic output of regression. Rather, path analysis allows one to examine the causal processes underlying the observed relationships and to estimate the relative importance of alternative paths of influence. The model testing permitted by path analysis further encourages a more explicitly causal approach in the search for explanations of the phenomena under investigation. Some actual examples of the use of path analysis should help make clearer the utility of the technique.

## Substantive Applications of Path Analysis

*The Transmission of Party Identification Across Generations:* The first example comes from the realm of political socialization and concerns the transmission of party identification across generations.[8] We will hypothesize a very simple three variable model in which the partisanship of parents is seen as the major determinant of the partisanship of the child. Determining the influence of fathers and mothers on the partisanship of their children is made more complicated by the fact that parents may influence each other politically as well as influencing their children. This suggests that the relationship between the parents might best be treated as reciprocal rather than recursive, but for the sake of exposition, the recursiveness of the example will be maintained. Since a number of earlier works on American political behavior, particularly in the context of partisan choice, suggested that the wife was more likely to follow her husband's lead than the reverse, the path of influence in our recursive model has been drawn from husband to wife, although a reciprocal linkage would be more appropriate. The reader should keep in mind that some of the subsequent results presented are a function of the initial decision to have father influence mother.

The basic model is depicted in Figure 11 along with the empirical correlations among the three variables. Note that there are no omitted linkages in the model; hence there are no tests of the model to be made. The data for this example come from the Jennings-Niemi socialization study of high school seniors in 1965. For a subset of the sample of seniors, the student and both parents were interviewed. Thus, we have independent reports of each family member's party identification which eliminates the possible distortions introduced when the child recalls his parents' partisanship. While party identification is measured as a seven point ordinal variable, Pearson r's have been computed. As a justification for violating the interval requirement, we might simply state at this stage that Monte Carlo simulations appear to indicate that no gross distortions will be introduced except in the most pathological of cases.

To solve for the direct effects $p_{21}$, $p_{31}$, and $p_{32}$, we can substitute the known correlations into the equations generated by the instrumental vari-

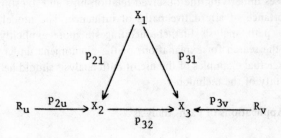

$X_1$ - father's partisanship

$X_2$ - mother's partisanship

$X_3$ - child's partisanship

(3.4)     $X_2 = p_{21}X_1 + p_{2u}R_u$

(3.5)     $X_3 = p_{31}X_1 + p_{32}X_2 + p_{3v}R_v$

Correlations:

|       | $X_2$ | $X_3$ |
|-------|-------|-------|
| $X_1$ | .71   | .57   |
| $X_2$ |       | .62   |

Figure 11:  The Basic Socialization Model

able technique and solve. Or we can simply regress $X_2$ on $X_1$ and $X_3$ on $X_1$ and $X_2$. The resulting estimates are:

$$p_{21} = .71$$
$$p_{31} = .27$$
$$p_{32} = .43$$

These results tell us that the direct effect of the mother's identification on the child is greater than the direct effect of the father. Since the path coefficients are standardized regression coefficients, we can make statements about a unit change in the standardized $X_1$ producing a .27 change in the standardized $X_3$.

The residual path coefficients can also be determined from regression analysis and are

$$p_{2u} = \sqrt{1 - r_{12}^2} = \sqrt{1 - (.71)^2} = .70$$

$$p_{3v} = \sqrt{1 - R_{3 \cdot 12}^2} = \sqrt{1 - (.65)^2} = .76$$

Note that the impact of $R_v$ on $X_3$ is substantially greater than the impact of the father or the mother. An alternative way of stating this is that only about 42% of the variance in the child's identification has been accounted for by the parents' identification. These results may seem unimpressive, even weak, to the reader who may wonder what happened to the 58% of the unexplained variance. Let me argue that these results are actually quite impressive, and that the reader, rather than worrying about the missing 58%, might do better to try to gain some sensitivity to the goodness of fit criteria associated with different analysis techniques.

For example, the comparison of the percentage difference in a contingency analysis with the $R^2$ in a regression analysis is highly illuminating. Percentage differences that are truly impressive (beyond 20 to 30%) in tabular analysis often translate into depressingly low $R^2$'s in the regression mode. This is particularly likely to occur with survey data which are characterized by substantial random measurement error which acts to decrease the fraction of explained variance. In our socialization example, the idea that there must be some variables out there which, if included in the model, would substantially increase the $R^2$ may sound plausible, but is just not the case. For example, inclusion of the child's friend's identification in the model increases the $R^2$ by less than 1%. What this suggests is that we should not impose unrealistically stringent criteria in assessing the goodness of our causal model. We, of course, always should be looking for important variables that we may have inadvertently ignored; however, we must also recognize that a variety of factors influence the magnitude of the $R^2$.

Using Wright's rules, we can decompose the correlations among the three variables as follows:

$$r_{12} = p_{21} \qquad\qquad [3.6]$$

$$r_{13} = p_{31} + p_{21}p_{32} \qquad\qquad [3.7]$$

$$r_{23} = p_{32} + p_{21}p_{31} \qquad\qquad [3.8]$$

A comparison of the empirical correlations with the numerical values of their decompositions shows that the two are equal; this occurs because there are no linkages omitted and hence no excess information (equations) that would allow for inconsistencies.

The term $p_{21}p_{32}$ in equation 3.7 represents the indirect effect of the father on the child via his impact on the mother. However, the term $p_{21}p_{31}$ in equation 3.8 does not represent the indirect impact of the mother on the child via her effect on the father since this violates the causal ordering among the variables; that is, according to our model, father influences mother and not the reverse. The term $p_{21}p_{31}$ is an example of a compound path that could be called a spurious effect as opposed to a substantively meaningful indirect effect.

We can summarize the various effects of the parents on the child as shown in Table 2. Whereas the mother had the greatest direct effect on the child, the father has the greater total effect. This result is clearly a function of the way we drew the linkage between father and mother; had the linkage been reversed, the mother would have been far more influential. Thus, the interpretation of indirect effects is on solid ground to the extent we are confident in the model we have posited.

We can extend the partisanship transmission model to a third generation by using the parental reports of their own parents' identification; this would yield the model of Figure 11 where for the sake of simplicity the grandfathers' identifications are included in the model. The double-headed curved arrow represents an unanalyzed correlation between exogenous variables.

One substantive question we might raise about the transmission of party identification is whether the grandparents have any direct influence on the child's partisanship or whether their impact is wholly mediated by the parents. This question can be answered by recourse to the Simon-Blalock technique. Since linkages were omitted between $X_4$ and $X_3$ and between $X_5$ and $X_3$, we would predict that $r_{34 \cdot 12} = 0$ and $r_{35 \cdot 12} = 0$ and compare the actual values to the predicted values.

**TABLE 2**
**Direct and Indirect Effects in the Transmission of Party Identification**

| Parent | Direct Effect | Indirect Effect | Total Effect |
|--------|--------|--------|--------|
| Father | .27 | .31 | .58 |
| Mother | .43 | --- | .43 |

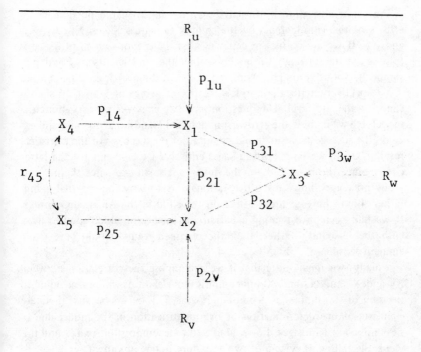

$X_1$ - father's identification

$X_2$ - mother's identification

$X_3$ - child's identification

$X_4$ - father's father's identification

$X_5$ - mother's father's identification

$$X_1 = p_{14}X_4 + p_{1u}R_u$$

$$X_2 = p_{21}X_1 + p_{25}X_5 + p_{2v}R_v$$

$$X_3 = p_{31}X_1 + p_{32}X_2 + p_{3w}R_w$$

Figure 12: The Transmission of Party Identification Across Three Generations

An easier and more informative way to check on the possible direct effects of the grandparents on the child is to regress $X_3$ on $X_1$, $X_2$, $X_4$, and $X_5$. If we are correct in believing that the grandparents' influence is fully mediated through the parents, then the coefficients $p_{34}$ and $p_{35}$ should be about zero. The estimated values of the coefficients are .12 and .03 respectively with the former coefficient achieving statistical significance at the .05 level. The question now becomes what to do about the model. Do we include the arrow from paternal grandfather to child and exclude the linkage from maternal grandfather on the basis of the statistical results? Or do we omit both linkages entirely? I would opt for the latter choice since the magnitude of the linkages is small *and* since there seems to be no compelling substantive rationale as to why the paternal grandfather should have a direct effect on the child in the American context. If we had been investigating a patriarchal society in which spouses lived with the husband's father, then the obtained results would have made eminent sense.

Finally, we might note that if we decompose the correlation between $X_4$ and $X_3$ and $X_5$ and $X_3$, the empirical correlations will not be equal to the sum of the simple and compound paths. This occurs because there are elements of overdetermination or overidentification in the model due to the omission of linkages. For example, the decomposition of $r_{14}$ and $r_{15}$ yields the following system of two equations in one unknown:

$$r_{14} = p_{14}$$

$$r_{15} = r_{45}p_{14}$$

By inspection the equations yield two estimates of $p_{14} - r_{14}$ and $r_{15}/r_{45}$ — and the estimates need not be consistent. The two estimates arise because of the omitted linkage between $X_1$ and $X_5$; had this linkage been included, the decomposition of $r_{14}$ and $r_{15}$ would have generated a system of two equations in the two unknowns $p_{14}$ and $p_{15}$. In general, when working with overdetermined models, it is likely that the various estimates of a coefficient will be at least slightly inconsistent. Where inconsistencies are slight, one can probably live with the model as it stands. But where inconsistencies are large, one might think about (among other things) revising one's model. Unfortunately, there are no hard and fast rules as to what constitutes a large versus a small inconsistency.

*Reanalysis of the Goldberg and the Miller and Stokes Data:* The uses of path analysis are further demonstrated by the following reanalysis of a part of Goldberg's (1966) work on voting behavior which was based on a probability sample of adult Americans. While Goldberg used the Simon-Blalock technique to test a series of models, he explicitly recognized the underlying regression justification and in fact presented beta coefficients for his last model. However, he did not make use of the estimated coefficients except to compare them with the corresponding partial r's. Hence we will take Goldberg's revised dual mediation model and show how a path analysis approach yields far more information. For clarity of presentation, we have omitted two weak linkages in Goldberg's final model. In addition, the path coefficients (standardized regression coefficients) reported in Figure 13 differ from Goldberg's but are based on the correlation matrix he presents in footnote 17 in his article.

There are a number of points to be made about Figure 13. Note that the most important, *immediate* determinant of respondent's vote is parti-

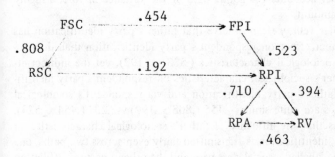

FSC — father's sociological characteristics

FPI — father's party identification

RSC — respondent's sociological characteristics

RPI — respondent's partisan identification

RPA — respondent's partisan attitudes

RV  — respondent's vote

Figure 13: A Modified Version of Goldberg's Revised Dual Mediation Model with Estimated Path Coefficients

san attitudes and not party identification. This does not mean, however, that partisan attitudes are overall more important than party identification for, according to the structure of the model, party identification has an indirect effect on vote via its impact on partisan attitudes. The various effects are shown in Table 3.

Although party identification has the weaker direct effect, it has the greater total effect. One should keep in mind that this result reflects the fact that the linkage between party identification and partisan attitudes went from the former to the latter. If we had little confidence in the justification for this linkage, we would have little confidence in our results. Thus, path analysis provides us with a numerical estimate of indirect and direct effects *after* we have specified the direction of the linkages. Estimating the residual path coefficient to respondent's vote yields a coefficient of .610 which suggests that unmeasured variables have a greater direct effect on vote than any one of the measured variables. Finally, the present model accounts for about 62% of the variance in vote, a highly respectable amount.

In a similar vein, we can observe that father's party identification has a greater direct effect on respondent's party identification than does respondent's sociological characteristics (.523 vs. 192), yet the indirect effects of father's sociological characteristics on respondent's party identification via father's party identification and via respondent's sociological characteristics are quite similar–.155 (.808 x .192) vs. .237 (.454 x .523). This suggests that the influence of father's sociological characteristics on child's party identification is transmitted fairly even across two paths, one that might be labelled a social class path and the other a partisan affiliation path.

As we did in the socialization example, we can use path analysis to test for the existence of linkages in a recursive model, our substantive vehicle this time being the recursive Miller and Stokes model depicted in Figure 10. As was argued in Chapter 1, the omission of the linkage between district attitudes and representative's behavior is essentially a theoretical assertion that there must be some intervening perceptual mechanisms in order for constituency attitudes to influence congressional behavior.

**TABLE 3**
**Effects of Party Identification and Partisan Attitudes on Vote**

|  | Direct Effect | Indirect Effect | Total Effect |
|---|---|---|---|
| Party Identification | .394 | .329 (.710 x .463) | .723 |
| Partisan Attitudes | .463 | ---- | .463 |

The omission of the linkage can be tested in two ways. One is to simply estimate its magnitude as if it were incorporated in the model. The resulting value of .075 lends credence to the reasoning underlying its omission. An alternative way of testing the linkage is to recognize that the correlation between any two variables can be decomposed into a sum of simple and compound paths. Figure 14 presents the estimated representation model; it is assumed that the linkage goes from perceptions to attitudes $(X_2$ to $X_3)$ and not the reverse. Note that there are three compound paths linking $X_1$ to $X_4$:

| Path | Value |
|------|-------|
| $p_{21}p_{42}$ | $.452 = (.738)(.613)$ |
| $p_{31}p_{43}$ | $.017 = (.052)(.327)$ |
| $p_{21}p_{32}p_{43}$ | $.146 = (.738)(.605)(.327)$ |

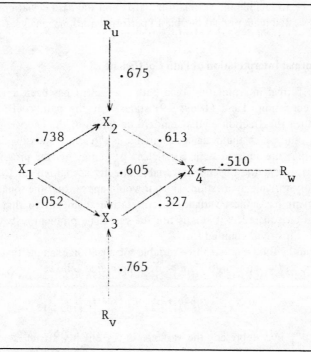

Figure 14: The Miller and Stokes Representation Model with Estimated Path Coefficients

The zero order correlation between $X_1$ and $X_4$ is .649; the sum of the three compound paths is .615. This very slight discrepancy (.649 − .615 = .034) again provides support for our decision to omit the linkage between $X_1$ and $X_4$.

The three compound paths calculated above help us specify the underlying processes whereby district attitudes influence elite behavior. For example, it is clear that the shared attitudes path of influence is very weak for civil rights, while the sanctions path is by far the strongest. Less interesting is the three step path which has perceptions influencing attitudes and not the reverse; the magnitude of this path of course reflects the assumption we made about the linkage between attitudes and perceptions.

Hopefully, these substantive examples have helped illuminate some of the advantages of path analysis. The Goldberg and Miller and Stokes illustrations suggest that much existing research and data can be profitably and readily reanalyzed from a more causal perspective. The only information needed to compute path coefficients is the correlations among the variables. To calculate path regression coefficients (unstandardized path coefficients), one also needs the standard deviations of the variables. This suggests that a helpful practice in reporting the results of one's research would be to include the correlation matrix and standard deviations so that the interested reader might be able to perform additional analyses.

### The Formal Interpretation of Path Coefficient

The formal interpretation of a path coefficient has been a source of some confusion. Land (1969: 8-9) states that the path coefficient $p_{ij}$ "measures the fraction of the standard deviation of the endogenous variable . . . for which the designated variable is *directly* responsible." Others assert that the squared path coefficient $p_{ij}^2$ represents the proportion of the variance in the dependent variable directly accounted for by the explanatory variable in question. Thus, it would appear that the squared path coefficient has a neat variance interpretation analogous to that for the correlation squared, but this is not the case. The problem rests with the phrase "directly accounted for."

It can be shown in our three variable socialization example that the variance in $X_3$ (which is unity) can be decomposed as follows:

$$\text{Var } X_3 = 1 = p_{31}^2 + p_{32}^2 + p_{3v}^2 + 2p_{31}p_{32}r_{12}$$

While $p_{31}^2$ may represent the variance in $X_3$ directly attributable to $X_1$, it does not represent the total variance in $X_3$ accounted for by $X_1$. The reason for this is the presence of the term $2p_{31}p_{32}r_{12}$ which stands for the portion of the variance in $X_3$ due to both $X_1$ and $X_2$, a quantity that cannot be uniquely distributed among $X_1$ and $X_2$. The only case in which we have an easy variance interpretation is when the term $2p_{31}p_{32}r_{12}$ is zero, when $r_{12} = 0$. But this degenerates into a simple regression model of direct effects only and is, therefore, a less interesting case than the one in which the explanatory variables themselves are causally related. If the problem of multicollinearity (to be discussed later) exists, it is possible for the path coefficients to exceed unity. Then one is in the untenable position of asserting that one variable directly accounted for more than 100% of the variance in the other variable.

There have been numerous efforts to partition variances into unique subsets, but these have been largely unconvincing. Duncan (1970: 38) puts this literature in proper perspective when he writes:

> Achieving an algebraically consistent partitioning or system of partialing is secondary in importance to setting up an appropriate representation (or "model") of the structure of the problem. Much confusion arises because of the protean character of regression and correlation statistics, which permits their algebraic manipulation into a large number of essentially equivalent but apparently distinct forms. Preoccupation with this algebra is not likely to generate anything new. . . . Even worse, it is likely to distract one from the more urgent task of making sure that the regression setup itself is suited to the inferences and interpretations to be attempted.

Even though Duncan violates his own advice, his argument is well stated. Thus, the most useful statements to be made in interpreting path coefficients involve a comparison of the relative magnitudes of the coefficients within the same model and an assertion that a certain change in one variable produces a specified change in another.

## Overidentification in Recursive Models

Whenever we leave out linkages in a recursive model, we end up generating more equations than unknowns, a system that is commonly referred to as overidentified or overdetermined. The problem becomes choosing a subset of equations for solving for the unknowns. What justification is there for choosing one set of equations over another? What reason is there to suggest, as was done earlier, that when there are extra instrumental variables available, one should use only those instruments that yield solutions equivalent to regression coefficients?

This is a problem that has concerned a number of investigators. Boudon (1968: 213-215) outlines a procedure involving the minimization of sums of squares for obtaining path estimates that utilizes the information provided by *all* equations. But Goldberger (1970) has shown that the estimates obtained by ordinary least squares are preferable to Boudon's since the former have smaller sampling variability. Goldberger's critique of Boudon's estimates emphasizes the need to explicitly lay out some desirable properties of estimators.

Wonnacott and Wonnacott (1970: 40-47) discuss some desirable properties of estimators. The first property considered is unbiasedness: an unbiased estimator is one that on the average gives the true population parameter. More formally, if $\theta$ is some unknown population parameter and $\hat{\theta}$ is an estimator of $\theta$, we say that $\hat{\theta}$ is an unbiased estimator of $\theta$ if $E(\hat{\theta}) = \theta$ where $E(\hat{\theta})$ is the expected value of the estimator $\hat{\theta}$. A second criterion in selecting an estimator is its efficiency. An efficient estimator is one that has a small sampling variability. That is, if we pick one sample and calculate an estimate, pick another sample and calculate an estimate, and so forth, the variance of the estimates should be small. Finally, a third property of an estimator is consistency. This is a weak criterion which states that $\hat{\theta}$ is consistent if $\hat{\theta} \rightarrow \theta$ as $n \rightarrow \infty$. What we are saying here is that the sample estimate should approach the true value as the sample size gets larger and larger. See Uslaner (1976) for a discussion of properties of estimators.

The Gauss-Markov Theorem (Wonnacott and Wonnacott, 1970: 21) states that within the class of linear unbiased estimators, the least squares estimators have minimum variance. What this means is there are no other linear unbiased estimators that are more efficient than the ordinary least squares estimators. In fact, the least squares estimates are often referred to as BLUE estimates—best (minimum variance), linear, unbiased estimates. This fact then provides some justification for using only those equations in solving that will yield estimates equivalent to regression coefficients. But this does not mean that the ordinary least squares estimates are better than all other possible estimates, only that they are better than any other linear unbiased estimate. But the property of being unbiased is not crucial or overriding. For example, consider the situation portrayed in Figure 15, in which we have the sampling distribution of two hypothetical estimators of $\theta - \hat{\theta}$ and $\hat{\hat{\theta}}$. Note that while $\hat{\theta}$ is unbiased (on the average yields the true value), its sampling variability is large so that any single estimate may be substantially different from the true value. Further observe that while $\hat{\hat{\theta}}$ is upwardly biased, its sampling variability is small so that it almost always yields estimates close to the true value. If one had to choose between $\hat{\theta}$ and $\hat{\hat{\theta}}$, one might very well opt for the biased estimator. This contrived example shows that while the ordinary least squares esti-

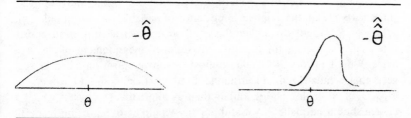

Figure 15: The Sampling Distribution of Two Hypothetical Estimators of Some Population Parameter

mates may be the minimum variance, unbiased estimates, one could at least imagine biased but more efficient estimators.

Thus, the problem of what to do with the excess information in over-identified recursive models is one of the major areas of investigation in recursive path estimation. Land (1973) has generalized the Gauss-Markov theorem for stochastic (as opposed to fixed) predictor variables. He has also shown (1973: 40) that single-equation maximum-likelihood estimators yield estimates numerically equivalent to the ordinary least square estimator and with very similar properties to the least squares estimates. He further shows (1973: 42) that "full-information maximum-likelihood estimation reduces to equation-by-equation least squares, provided that there are no cross-equation constraints on the coefficients." Finally, Land presents a test statistic (1973: 45-47) that can be employed in testing hypotheses about the omitted linkages in an overidentified model. It should be noted that Land requires his estimates to be unbiased, efficient, and consistent, or their asymptotic equivalents.

## Additional Problems in Path Analysis

*Standardized vs. Unstandardized Coefficients:* The use of standardized vs. unstandardized coefficients has sparked a major controversy (Blalock, 1967; Forbes and Tufte, 1968; Tukey, 1954; Turner and Stevens, 1959; Wright, 1960). As is often the case in such controversies, common sense and not formal rules seems to provide the best guide as to how to proceed. It seems that the best rule of thumb in choosing one coefficient over another is the kind of statement one wants to make. If one wants to make comparisons *across* subsets of data—such as blacks vs. whites or South vs. non-South—then unstandardized coefficients are preferable (assuming the variables are measured on a determinate scale) since they are immune to the effects of the different variances in the same variable that may arise due to subsetting. In short, when making comparisons across populations, the unstandardized estimates merit investigation. But if one wants to make statements about the relative importance of variables *within* populations or subsets of populations, then the standardized coefficient is more appropriate since it adjusts for the different scales of measurement of the variables. Wright (1960: 202) takes a most reasonable position when he suggests that standardized and unstandardized coefficients should be seen "as aspects of a single theory, rather than as alternatives between which a choice should be made." A useful practice would be to report both coefficients, or if one reports only one coefficient, present the standard deviations of the variables so that the reader can retrieve the other coefficient since the standardized coefficient is equal to the unstandardized coefficient times the ratio of the standard deviation of the independent variable to the standard deviation of the dependent variable. That is, $B_{21} = (b_{21})(\sigma_{x_1}/\sigma_{x_2})$ where B is the standardized coefficient and b the unstandardized coefficient.

*Multicollinearity:* The problem of multicollinearity—highly correlated independent variables—has received extensive treatment (Deegan, 1972; Blalock, 1963; Farrar and Glauber, 1967). The presence of high levels of collinearity leads to sizable standard errors of the estimated regression coefficients. This means that if we were to draw another sample from the same population and reestimate the equation, our new estimates might be substantially different—even though in both cases they had the desirable properties of regression estimates discussed previously. Thus, multicollinearity makes it difficult to make causal inferences since the path estimates can differ dramatically from one sample to another.

Since multicollinearity is a problem arising from the instability of sample estimates, some investigators argue that researchers working with the entire population (that is, all the nations of the world or the 50 American states) need not worry about the problem. There are two arguments against accepting this position too uncritically. One is that populations may not be as well-defined as one thinks. When a new nation comes into existence, the population has changed, and if multicollinearity is present, the addition of the new unit to the analysis can radically change the obtained regression estimates, certainly a discomforting situation. Furthermore, if one collects data from a set of units at a single time point, one might want to argue that one has in effect picked a sample of the potential universe of observations, where the universe is defined not only by cases and variables, but also by a time dimension.

Multicollinearity is more likely to be a problem with aggregate data than with survey (individual) data since in aggregating observations, the random measure error component of the scores is likely to be cancelled, whereas in survey data, random measurement error is ever present. And, as mentioned earlier, the presence of random error attenuates correlation coefficients, thereby making the problem of collinearity less likely. Deegan (1972) shows that large sample sizes can reduce the impact of collinearity which also makes collinearity less worrisome in survey data than in aggregate data. It is not uncommon to have survey samples of over 1,500 respondents, while our number of aggregate units is usually much smaller such as the 50 American states, the 90 French departments, or the 150+ nations of the world. Deegan (1972) presents a technique—ridge regression with multiple samples—to surmount the problems of collinearity; unfortunately in the social sciences, we are not very often in the position of having multiple samples available.

## IDENTIFICATION AND NONRECURSIVE ESTIMATION

### An Intuitive Look at Identification

Before formally discussing identification, it may be helpful to consider the topic from an intuitive perspective by employing analogies to algebraic systems of equations. If we think of the problem of identification as having sufficient information to come up with a unique solution(s) for a set of unknowns, then we might by analogy say that equations 3.9 and 3.10 below represent an exactly identified system since there are just as many linearly independent equations as unknowns, thereby yielding the unique solution set X = 2 and Y = 1.

$$2X + 3Y = 7 \qquad [3.9]$$
$$X - 4Y = -2 \qquad [3.10]$$

Equations 3.11 and 3.12 might be considered an underidentified system since there are fewer linearly independent equations than unknowns. That is, while there are two equations in two unknowns, the second equation is simply a multiple of the first which means that it does not contribute any information in solving for X and Y. Hence, we in effect have one equation in two unknowns. This means that an infinite set of solutions exists; for example, X = 2 and Y = 1, X = 3.5 and Y = 0, and X = 5 and Y = -1 are all solution sets for equations 3.11 and 3.12. If we are trying to come up with interpretable estimates of some unknowns, then the situation of infinite solutions is obviously fatal to any sound inferences.

$$2X + 3Y = 7 \qquad\qquad [3.11]$$
$$4X + 6Y = 14 \qquad\qquad [3.12]$$

Finally, equations 3.13-3.15 can be viewed as an overidentified system since there are more equations than unknowns. If we used equations 3.13 and 3.14 to solve, we would get $X = 3$ and $Y = -1$. Equations 3.13 and 3.15 generate solutions of $X = 12$ and $Y = 17$, while equations 3.14 and 3.15 yield $X = 6/11$ and $Y = -2/11$. While there is only a finite set of solutions here, it still is the case that different pairs of equations give very dissimilar results, again an unsatisfactory situation for making inferences on the basis of the estimates. In equations 3.13-3.15, the excess equation is not consistent with the other two.

$$2X - Y = 7 \qquad\qquad [3.13]$$
$$X + 3Y = 0 \qquad\qquad [3.14]$$
$$3X - 2Y = 2 \qquad\qquad [3.15]$$

## Identification in Recursive Systems

In our discussion of recursive estimation, we never formally treated the topic of identification. This was not because identification is an irrelevant concern in recursive models; rather it was due to the fact that in the recursive case we make a number of assumptions that guarantee that our equations will be identified.

There are two basic ways of identifying a system of equations: one is by imposing limitations on the coefficients linking measured variables; the other is by making certain assumptions about the correlations among the residual terms. These are generally called coefficient and covariance restrictions. In a recursive model, we always make many coefficient restrictions since we have set at least half of our coefficients equal to zero. For example, if in a recursive model we have said that $X_1$ influences $X_2$ (represented by $P_{21}$), we have implicitly set $P_{12}$ equal to zero. Furthermore, in the recursive case, we are willing to make assumptions about error terms which, while unrealistic, are not contradicted by the structure of the model. Whenever we make our usual assumptions about residual terms in a recursive model, we are guaranteed that our system of equations will be at least identified (Boudon, 1968: 205). In the nonrecursive case, we impose fewer restrictions upon the coefficients and covariances, thereby leading to more unknowns and greater difficulty in obtaining unique solutions.

Covariance and coefficient restrictions can be illustrated by examining a three variable nonrecursive model discussed by Simon (1957: 41-43) and presented in Figure 16. Note that we have here three equations in nine unknowns (six unknown path coefficients and three unobservable errors), clearly a case of underidentification or insufficient information to solve. Yet when we worked with three variable models before (such as the socialization example), we were able to solve for the paths. This was accomplished by our making both coefficient and covariance restrictions. In the former category, we assumed a recursive model. This meant that three coefficients were set equal to zero which left us with a system of three equations in six unknowns. We also introduced three covariance restrictions by assuming that the three residual terms were pairwise uncorrelated. This eliminated three more unknowns and left us with a system of three equations in three unknowns which was solvable.

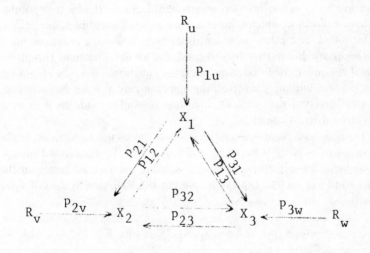

$$(3.16) \qquad X_1 = p_{12}X_2 + p_{13}X_3 + p_{1u}R_u$$

$$(3.17) \qquad X_2 = p_{21}X_1 + p_{23}X_3 + p_{2v}R_v$$

$$(3.18) \qquad X_3 = p_{31}X_1 + p_{32}X_2 + p_{3w}R_w$$

Figure 16: A Three Variable Nonrecursive Model and Structural Equations

## Identification in Nonrecursive Systems

As was shown in Chapter 2 in our discussion of equations 2.11 and 2.12, the assumptions we make in the recursive case about the covariances among the residual variables are clearly incorrect in the nonrecursive situation. In fact, one advantageous feature of nonrecursive models is that they are more realistic since they do not require that the residual variables be uncorrelated. But this gain in realism means that covariance restrictions will not be as helpful in identifying a system of equations in nonrecursive models as they were in recursive models. Thus, in nonrecursive models, investigators most often talk of two coefficient restrictions—the rank and order conditions—in identifying a model.

*The Order Condition:* The order condition states that if we have a model consisting of $k$ linear equations, then for any equation in that model to be identified, it must excluded at least $k-1$ of the variables that appear in the model. Note that with the order condition, one makes an equation by equation decision about identification. Hence, it is possible to have a model in which some equations are underidentified, some exactly identified, and others overidentified. Technically, the order condition is a necessary, but not a sufficient condition for identification. This means that if the order condition is not met, the equation will not be identified. But if the condition is satisfied, the equation may still not be identified. In most practical data analysis situations, the order condition is a necessary and sufficient condition.

To show how the order condition works, let us use as an example the nonrecursive version of the Miller and Stokes model presented in Figure 4. If we write the structural equations isolating the residual terms on the right hand side of the expression, we get the following system of three equations.

$$-p_{21}X_1 + \quad X_2 - p_{23}X_3 \qquad = p_{2u}R_u \qquad [3.19]$$

$$-p_{31}X_1 - p_{32}X_2 + \quad X_3 \qquad = p_{3v}R_v \qquad [3.20]$$

$$-p_{42}X_2 - p_{43}X_3 + X_4 = p_{4w}R_w \qquad [3.21]$$

To check whether equations 3.19-3.21 satisfy the order condition, it is easiest to inspect the matrix of coefficients and look for zero coefficients which mean that variables have been omitted. The matrix of coefficients for equations 3.19-3.21 looks like:

$$\begin{bmatrix} -p_{21} & 1 & -p_{23} & 0 \\ -p_{31} & -p_{32} & 1 & 0 \\ 0 & -p_{42} & -p_{43} & 1 \end{bmatrix}$$

The three rows of the matrix refer to the three structural equations, while the four columns correspond to our four measured variables $X_1$, $X_2$, $X_3$, and $X_4$. Thus, the coefficient $-p_{21}$ in the matrix refers to the coefficient of $X_1$ in equation 3.19.

According to the order condition, for equations 3.19-3.21 to be identified, they must exclude at least two ($k - 1 = 3 - 1 = 2$) variables. Inspection of the coefficient matrix shows that none of the equations meets the order condition; equation 3.19 and 3.20 each exclude only one variable—$X_4$, while equation 3.21 also excludes only one variable—$X_1$. Thus, none of the equations in the nonrecursive model are identified and therefore meaningful estimates of the coefficients cannot be obtained.

An alternative version of the order condition is given by Wonnacott and Wonnacott; their version is appropriate when the structural equations are written in our usual way with the dependent variable isolated on the left hand side of the expression. They write (1970: 180) that for an equation to be identified "the number of exogenous variables excluded from the equation must at least equal the number of endogenous variables included on the right-hand side of the equation." This statement of the order condition is particularly useful when we try to identify equations by introducing new exogenous variables to our system, a topic developed shortly.

*The Rank Condition:* The rank condition states (Christ, 1966: 320) that an equation in a model of k linear equation is identified if and only if at least one nonzero determinant[9] of $k - 1$ rows and columns is contained in the matrix of coefficients of the structural equations remaining after omitting all columns of coefficients not having a zero entry in the equation in question and omitting the row of coefficients of that equation. Note again that decisions about identification are made on an equation by equation basis. If more than one nonzero determinant can be found, then the equation in question is overidentified. The rank condition is a necessary and sufficient condition.

To illustrate the use of the rank condition, let us again examine the equations of the nonrecursive Miller and Stokes model even though the failure of the equations to satisfy the order condition tells us that they are underidentified. In order for equations 3.19-3.21 to satisfy the rank condition, we must be able to find nonzero determinants of order two by two ($k - 1 = 2$) embedded within the matrix of coefficients on page 53 by following the steps outlined in the rank condition. For equation 3.19, we would omit from the matrix of coefficients the coefficients of equation 3.19 and wherever these coefficients were nonzero we would also strike out the corresponding columns of coefficients. Then we would search for at least one nonzero determinant of two rows and two columns from among the remaining coefficients; if we could find such a determinant, then equation 3.19 would be identified. When the appropriate coefficients for equation 3.19 are eliminated, the only elements remaining are

$$\begin{bmatrix} 0 \\ 1 \end{bmatrix},$$

which is obviously not a nonzero, two by two determinant; hence equation 3.19 is not identified. Similar results obtain for equations 3.20 and 3.21 as our previous application of the order condition led us to expect.

## Nonrecursive Estimation and Levels of Identification

*Underidentification:* Given that the rank and order conditions tell us whether our equations are underidentified, exactly identified, or overidentified, the question becomes how to obtain estimates of our unknown coefficients for each level of identification. When an equation is underidentified, there is no estimation technique available that yields satisfactory estimates; attempts to use common estimation techniques will generally result in biased and inconsistent estimates. Thus, one must try to convert an underidentified equation to an identified one by introducing new variables into one's model.

While theoretical and substantive concerns play the major role in the search for these new variables, there are certain desirable statistical properties that these new variables should possess. First, they should be exogenous, uncorrelated with the residual terms associated with the endogenous variables. Furthermore, they should be strongly correlated with the variables upon which they are impinging. Justification for these conditions is provided by Fisher (1971).

Let us imagine in the Miller and Stokes example that we could find two new exogenous variables $X_5$ and $X_6$ that behaved as depicted in Figure 17. The structural equations and matrix of coefficients for this revised model are given below.

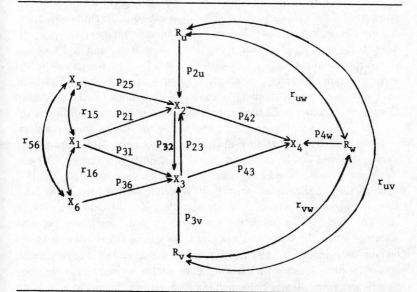

**Figure 17: The Nonrecursive Miller and Stokes Representation Model with Two Hypothetical Exogenous Variables**

$$-p_{21}X_1 + X_2 - p_{23}X_3 - p_{25}X_5 \qquad = p_{2u}R_u \qquad [3.22]$$

$$-p_{31}X_1 - p_{32}X_2 + X_3 \qquad\qquad - p_{36}X_6 = p_{3v}R_v \qquad [3.23]$$

$$-p_{42}X_2 - p_{43}X_3 + X_4 \qquad\qquad\qquad = p_{4w}R_w \qquad [3.24]$$

$$\begin{bmatrix} -p_{21} & 1 & -p_{23} & 0 & -p_{25} & 0 \\ -p_{31} & -p_{32} & 1 & 0 & 0 & -p_{36} \\ 0 & -p_{42} & -p_{43} & 1 & 0 & 0 \end{bmatrix}$$

Note that the addition of $X_5$ and $X_6$ to the model does not change the number of equations. Hence, the order condition requires that each equation excludes $k-1$ variables where k refers to the number of linear equations, in this case three. Thus, all three equations satisfy the order condition since they all exclude at least two $(k-1)$ variables. And by the rank condition, equations 3.22 and 3.23 are exactly identified since we can find a nonzero two by two determinant for each equation, while equation 3.24 is overidentified since more than one nonzero determinant can be found.[10]

Note that each of our hypothetical new exogenous variables influences only one of the endogenous variables involved in the reciprocal linkage; $X_5$ directly influences only $X_2$, while $X_6$ directly impinges upon $X_3$. If, instead, $X_5$ and $X_6$ each directly influenced *both* $X_2$ and $X_3$, then the structural equations for $X_2$ and $X_3$ would still have been underidentified as can be quickly seen by application of the order condition. Thus, not only must we find substantively meaningful exogenous variables; in addition, these variables must have specific patterns of interrelationships with the endogenous variables in order to help solve the identification problem.

If we actually wanted to estimate the nonrecursive Miller and Stokes model, it would not be sufficient simply to identify new variables $X_5$ and $X_6$; these variables would also have to be measured in the data set. This requires that at the design stage of the research the need for $X_5$ and $X_6$ was recognized and plans were made to collect observations on each variable. As nonrecursive modeling was certainly not familiar to political scientists when the data were collected, no special efforts were made to include measures of $X_5$ and $X_6$. Hence, all the secondary analyst can do now is search through the existing data set for satisfactory exogenous variables; needless to say, the search is a difficult one.

The reader can verify for himself that the three variable socialization of party identification model is underidentified when the reciprocal linkage is included between father's partisanship and mother's partisanship. However, here we are in much better shape in finding exogenous variables to identify the system of equations. In fact, two substantively and statistically satisfying exogenous variables have already been discussed—the partisanship of the maternal and paternal grandfathers. The reader can again verify for himself that in the nonrecursive socialization model portrayed in Figure 18, the equations for $X_1$, $X_2$, and $X_3$ are exactly identified. Note that $X_4$ influences only $X_1$ and $X_5$ only $X_2$; if $X_4$ and $X_5$ had direct influences on *both* $X_1$ and $X_2$, the equations for $X_1$ and $X_2$ would still have been underidentified. The decision to have $X_4$ directly affect only $X_1$ (and $X_5$ only $X_2$) is a substantive one that asserts that in the American context there is little reason to believe that the father-in-law has any substantial impact whatsoever on the partisanship of his son-in-law or daughter-in-law.

*Exact Identification:* If a nonrecursive system is identified, then there are a variety of estimation techniques that one can use without an extensive econometrics background. For example, there is an instrumental variable procedure available for nonrecursive, exactly identified systems similar to the instrumental variable technique for recursive models. The basic

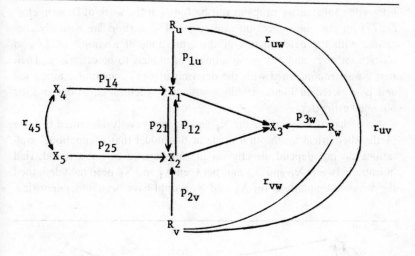

(3.25) $\quad X_1 = p_{14}X_4 + p_{12}X_2 + p_{1u}R_u$

(3.26) $\quad X_2 = p_{25}X_5 + p_{21}X_1 + p_{2v}R_v$

(3.27) $\quad X_3 = p_{31}X_1 + p_{32}X_2 + p_{3w}R_w$

$X_1$ - father's identification

$X_2$ - mother's identification

$X_3$ - child's identification

$X_4$ - father's father's identification

$X_5$ - mother's father's identification

Figure 18: The Nonrecursive Socialization Model and Structural Equations

difference between the two is that in the nonrecursive case one operates on the structural equations with exogenous variables only, whether or not they appear in the equation under investigation. For example, equation 3.25 is exactly identified: to solve for $p_{14}$ and $p_{12}$, one would use as instruments $X_4$ and $X_5$ which would yield two equations in two unknowns. This instrumental variable technique gives results identical to indirect least squares (ILS) and two stage least squares (2SLS), a topic to be covered shortly.

A clear example of the instrumental variable procedure applied to an interesting substantive problem can be found in the work of Duncan et al. (1971) on peer influences on aspirations. The authors are basically concerned with the determinants of the aspirations of a sample of 17-year old school boys and lay out a number of models to be estimated. Their first model is concerned with the determinants of occupational aspiration and is depicted in Figure 19 along with the structural equations and the obtained estimates.

Note that the equations for $X_5$ and $X_6$ are exactly identified because of the theoretical assumption made in the model that occupational aspirations do not depend directly on the intelligence of one's friend. Had linkages between $X_1$ and $X_6$ and between $X_4$ and $X_5$ been included, then the structural equations for $X_5$ and $X_6$ would have been underidentified.

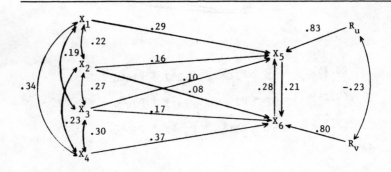

$$(3.28) \quad X_5 = p_{51}X_1 + p_{52}X_2 + p_{53}X_3 + p_{56}X_6 + p_{5u}R_u$$

$$(3.29) \quad X_6 = p_{62}X_2 + p_{63}X_3 + p_{64}X_4 + p_{65}X_5 + p_{6v}R_v$$

$X_1$ - intelligence

$X_2$ - family SES

$X_3$ - friend's family SES

$X_4$ - friend's intelligence

$X_5$ - occupational aspiration

$X_6$ - friend's occupational aspiration

Figure 19: An Exactly Identified Model: Peer Influences on Aspirations

Note further that $R_u$ and $R_v$ are allowed to be correlated and that the only covariance restrictions involve zero intercorrelations between the exogenous and the residual variables. The actual estimates were obtained by multiplying equation 3.28 by the four exogenous variables, taking expected values and simplifying, resulting in a system of four equations in the four unknowns $p_{51}$, $p_{52}$, $p_{53}$, and $p_{56}$. A similar procedure was used to solve for the unknowns of equation 3.29.

Substantively, one might conclude that the impact of family SES and friend's family SES on occupational aspirations is quite weak, while the influence of intelligence and peers' occupational aspirations is somewhat greater. Duncan et al. detail how the correlation between the residual variables can be calculated; it suffices to note that the procedure is a tedious one not amenable to hand calculation. The authors suggest that the correlation between the residual variables can serve as a test of the model, that a sizable negative correlation between residual variables that are associated with positively correlated endogenous variables may mean that inadequacies of the model are being forced into the residual terms. More work is needed on the interpretation of the correlations among residual variables.

When the interrelationships among our variables are viewed as reciprocal, we must construct and estimate an explicitly reciprocal model rather than examine two (or more) recursive models. This can be illustrated by returning to our socialization of partisanship example and comparing the results obtained with a reciprocal linkage between mother and father with the results gotten by estimating two recursive models—one in which father influences mother, the other in which mother influences father. If we take the model presented in Figure 18 and omit the linkage from $X_2$ to $X_1$, the estimate for $p_{21}$—the father's impact on the mother—is about .64. Likewise, if we omit the linkage from $X_1$ to $X_2$, then the estimate for $p_{12}$—the mother's impact on the father—is about .57. When both linkages are simultaneously included in the nonrecursive model, the obtained estimates for $p_{21}$ and $p_{12}$ are about .6 and .3 respectively. Thus, in the recursive models, the effects of father on mother and mother on father are approximately equal; while in the nonrecursive case, the father's influence on the mother's partisanship is almost twice the mother's effect on the father. These results demonstrate that substantively inaccurate results can be generated by the failure to build directly into one's model the reciprocal relationships that one believes exist. More information about the estimation and interpretation of the nonrecursive socialization model can be found in the work of Rabinowitz (1969) and Karns (1973).

*Overidentification:* With overidentified equations, the question of what to do with excess information again arises. A number of estimation strategies are available; one that is readily understandable and yields consistent estimates is two stage least squares. Consider the following model and structural equations depicted in Figure 20. Note that equation 3.30 is exactly identified and could therefore be estimated by the instrumental variable procedure discussed above (as well as by two stage least squares), while equation 3.31 is overidentified since we have three exogenous variables that could be used as instruments to estimate only two unknowns— $p_{53}$ and $p_{54}$.

One might argue that we should use as our instruments those two with the highest correlations with $X_5$ à la one of Fisher's (1971) suggestions about choosing instrumental variables. However, the situation becomes more complicated when we recognize that while our exogenous variables may be uncorrelated with the residual terms in the population, in any sample of observations that we pick from the population, there may be a nonzero, albeit small correlation between the exogenous and residual variables. Thus, while there may be a unique solution to the system of three equations in two unknowns generated by all three instruments for the population, there may be no solution for the sample that satisfies all three equations simultaneously. Different subsets of two equations each may yield different results. Hence, we turn to two stage least squares as an estimation technique that utilizes all the information (instruments) simultaneously.

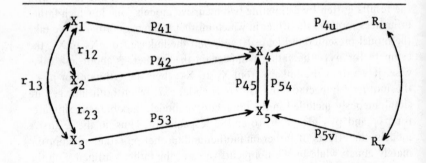

$$(3.30) \quad X_4 = p_{41}X_1 + p_{42}X_2 + p_{45}X_5 + p_{4u}R_u$$

$$(3.31) \quad X_5 = p_{53}X_3 + p_{54}X_4 + p_{5v}R_v$$

Figure 20: Overidentification and Two Stage Least Squares

Basically, 2SLS involves two successive applications of ordinary least squares. As equations 3.30 and 3.31 now stand, one cannot simply regress $X_4$ on $X_1$, $X_2$, and $X_5$, and $X_5$ on $X_3$ and $X_4$ since $X_5$ and $R_u$ are correlated in equation 3.30 and $X_4$ and $R_v$ are correlated in equation 3.31. Thus, the first stage in 2SLS is to regress $X_4$ and $X_5$ on $X_1$, $X_2$, and $X_3$ (a proper regression), obtaining two new variables $\hat{X}_4$ and $\hat{X}_5$. Since $\hat{X}_4$ and $\hat{X}_5$ are linear combinations of variables that are themselves uncorrelated with $R_u$ and $R_v$, then $\hat{X}_4$ and $\hat{X}_5$ are also uncorrelated with $R_u$ and $R_v$. This means we can now regress $X_4$ on $X_1$, $X_2$, and $\hat{X}_5$ and $X_5$ on $X_3$ and $\hat{X}_4$; this is the second stage of 2SLS. Two stage least squares is a useful estimation technique since it is appropriate for exactly identified and overidentified equations and is finally becoming available in packages of computer programs.

## SUMMATION

The essentials of recursive and nonrecursive path estimation have now been set out. It should be apparent to the reader that many important topics have merely been touched upon while others have been avoided altogether. For example, our exposition of techniques and examples has focused mainly on static, cross-sectional models, yet there is an extensive literature on time series and dynamic analysis that merits attention for appropriate substantive problems. For the potential causal modeller who wishes to acquire additional skills and depth in the area, a profitable course of action to follow is formal training in econometrics. Many of the crucial issues remaining in path analysis—such as optimal estimation techniques for overidentified systems of equations—are central concerns to econometricians.

Yet one need not be a formally trained econometrician to apply the techniques discussed herein properly. In most instances, computer programs are available to perform the dirty work of generating estimates. However, any results, whether computer or hand-generated, can only be as convincing as the data and theory underlying the causal model. Problems of indicator validity cannot be overlooked nor can questions about model specification be glossed over. Hence we again come back to our earlier assertion that serious errors in the construction and evaluation of causal models are more likely to be due to mistakes made in those stages of the research process prior to data analysis.

# 4. CONCLUSIONS

## SOME ADDITIONAL CONCERNS

The purpose of this paper has been to present some techniques appropriate for the causal analysis of data. Only a limited set of techniques appropriate for interval data has been considered, although as mentioned in Chapter 1, there is a growing body of literature on causal analysis with nominal and ordinal data (Goodman, 1970, 1972, 1973; Lehnen and Koch, 1973, 1974). The techniques discussed herein generally assumed linear and additive relationships, although there are increasing examples of non-additive relationships (Blalock, 1965; Blalock, 1968: 178-186) and the use of transformations to convert nonlinear equations into linear ones that are amenable to ordinary least squares procedures (Wonnacott and Wonnacott, 1970: 91-98; Strouse and Williams, 1972). Furthermore, as mentioned earlier, the techniques covered herein were mainly static, appropriate primarily for cross-sectional data; currently, simultaneous equation causal techniques (as contrasted to differential equation and simulation and dynamic modeling efforts) suitable for panel data are gaining wider circulation (Pelz and Andrews, 1964; Duncan, 1969; Heise, 1970). Finally, only one estimation technique for overidentified, nonrecursive systems (two stage least squares) has been presented, although the work of Karns (1974) suggests that 2SLS is generally to be preferred over other estimation techniques such as limited information maximum likelihood on grounds of ease of use and robustness, particularly in the presence of specification errors.

In addition to the topics listed above, there are two areas of ongoing research that are of particular relevance to those contemplating the use of the path analysis techniques described in Chapter 3. The first area is a causal analysis of the consequences of measurement error, while the second is an analysis of the effects of employing the techniques discussed herein with ordinal data, thereby violating the interval data assumption. Each of these topics will be briefly discussed.

## Measurement Error

The causal analysis of measurement error can be subsumed under the more general heading of path analysis with unmeasured or unobserved variables, a topic that is receiving increased attention (Land, 1970; Hauser and Goldberger, 1971; Werts, Jöreskog and Linn, 1973; Wiley, 1973). We shall examine two cases in which unmeasured variables appear as causes of measured variables in path diagrams.

By measurement error is meant any deviation from the true value of a variable that arises in the measurement process. In symbolic notation we say that $X' = T + e$ where T is the true variable (without measurement error), $X'$ is the measured variable or indicator of the true variable and e the measurement error. This equation can be represented by the simple diagram $T \longrightarrow X' \longleftarrow e$.

Measurement errors may be random or nonrandom. If random, the error is just as likely to be above the true value as below, and the expected value of the sum of all errors for any single variable will be zero. More importantly, the measurement errors are assumed to be uncorrelated with the true scores. Nonrandom error refers to a systematic upward or downward bias in the observations; in the single indicator case, the errors of measurement and true scores will be correlated. Of the two kinds of errors, random is less worrisome for two reasons. Techniques for estimating the effects of random error are better developed and the consequences of random error can often be identified more confidently. For example, in calculating bivariate correlation and regression coefficients, random error attenuates the results, and, unless this attenuation is corrected, random error leads to overly conservative and cautious statements of bivariate relationships. Nonrandom error, on the other hand, can bias coefficients either upward or downward. Once we leave the bivariate case and move to the more complex multivariate situation, the attenuating effects of random measurement error are less easily estimated. As Blalock et al. (1970: 78) observe in the regression context:

> Any random measurement errors in the *independent* variables will produce attenuating biases in the ordinary least-squares estimates, the degree of bias being dependent on the relative magnitudes of the measurement error variance as compared with the variance in the independent variable concerned. Where there are several independent variables, this in effect means that there will be differential attenuations that will imply trouble whenever one wishes to sort out the component effects of each independent variable.

There are three basic path analysis techniques for assessing the consequences of measurement error, each of which requires a different kind of information. One approach requires measures of the same variables from the same units at multiple points in time such as panel data (Heise, 1971; Wiley and Wiley, 1971), while a second employs multiple indicators of the same variables (Costner, 1971). A third approach requires knowledge about the true scores of the variables (Siegel and Hodge, 1968), a requirement that we very often cannot meet. Finally, there are some non-path-analytic techniques for determining the consequences of measurement error (Blalock et al., 1970).

That measurement error does exist in our data has been amply demonstrated. For example, Asher (1974: 474) found that between one-half to 1% of the respondents in the Survey Research Center's three wave (1956, 1958, 1960) American panel study were not assigned to the same sex category at two successive point in time. Furthermore, it was found (Asher, 1974: 474) that in comparing the 1956-1958 and the 1958-1960 reports on education, 13.4 and 12.5% of the respondents (150 of 1,118 for 1956-1958, and 174 of 1,396 for 1958-1960) were assigned a lower level of education at the *later* time point, obviously evidence of substantial error since an individual's level of education presumably cannot decrease over time.

The multiple indicators and the observations over time strategies were employed by Asher to evaluate the consequences of random measurement error in the measurement of party identification. The Jennings-Niemi socialization study which contained independent reports from husbands and wives on the same variables provided the data for the multiple indicators analysis, while the Survey Research Center's American panel study provided the data for the observations over time work. The path diagrams underlying each analysis are presented in Figures 21 and 22, while the results of the analyses are presented in Table 4.

The reader can observe that in all cases the correction for the attenuating effects of random measurement error exceeded .1. While this may not seem exceedingly worrisome, one should keep in mind that party identification is relatively well defined and measured; with other, less well measured variables, the consequences of measurement error are likely to be much greater. In short, measurement error concerns cannot safely be ignored in most instances.

## Treating Ordinal Data as Interval

In this section, we will discuss some research that examines the consequences of violating the interval data requirement, for example, by calculating product-moment correlations and regression coefficients on ordinal data. The question of how readily one can and should treat ordinal data as interval has sparked a major controversy. On the one hand, some investigators (Wilson, 1971) argue that ordinal-based results where interval data are actually required will be inconclusive since some legitimate transformation of the ordinal observations will reverse the conclusions reached. For such investigators, a prime goal of social research is the construction of reliable and valid interval level measures prior to model testing. Other investigators (Bohrnstedt and Carter, 1971; Labovitz, 1967, 1970) believe that the absence of interval data should not prevent one from proceeding with model testing and parameter estimation. It is argued that treating ordinal variables as if they were interval allows one to employ more powerful and sophisticated statistical techniques. Often, work with contrived or simulated data is cited to demonstrate that ordinal data can be analyzed by techniques that formally require interval data without any serious distortions.

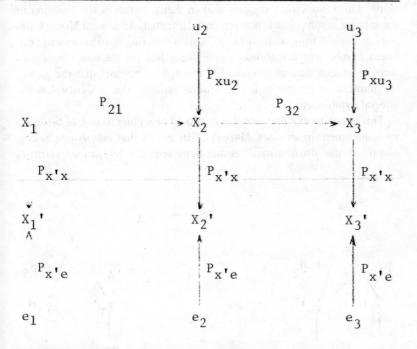

**Figure 21: A Three-Wave Model of Party Identification**

$X_1$, $X_2$, and $X_3$ represent the true party identification in 1956, 1958, and 1970 respectively, while $X_1'$, $X_2'$, and $X_3'$ represent the measured party identification at the same time points. The $e_i$'s are random variables representing measurement error, while the $u_i$'s are disturbance terms that have influenced the $X_i$'s in the time interval. A number of assumptions are made in Figure 21:

(1) the measurement errors at different time points are uncorrelated;

(2) the measurement errors are uncorrleated with the true scores (the $X_i$'s);

(3) the disturbance term at any time point is uncorrelated with the value of $X_i$ at previous time points; and

(4) the relationship between the true variable $X_i$ and its indicator $X_i'$ is constant over time, represented by the same coefficient $p_{x'x}$ assigned to the three linkages between the true and measured party identification.

It is difficult to reconcile these arguments, although I come down more favorably on the side of those who are less worried about violating the interval assumption. While it is certainly correct that any set of ordinal-based results can be upset by applying the appropriate transformation to one's data, it seems to me that one should not automatically assume that it is the most pathological of situations that one is confronting. Although some transformation could alter one's results, this does not mean that the results obtained are incorrect or off the mark. There has been ample Monte Carlo work that suggests that in many instances the violation of the interval assumption is not very consequential. Additional Monte Carlo work is needed using ordinal variables with differing distributions and different numbers of categories to give one a feel for the consequences of treating ordinal data as interval. For example, it appears that the greater the number of categories in the ordinal variable, the less critical is the interval requirement.

This is not to say that one can or should be willing to violate the interval requirement in all cases. Mayer (1970) asserts that one should be cognizant of the distributional assumptions required by various statistics

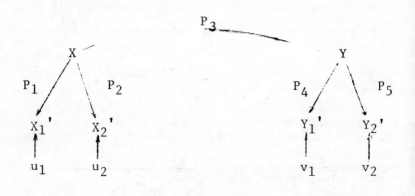

**Figure 22: A Two Indicator Model of Party Identification**

X and Y represent the true party identification of the husband and wife respectively, while $X_1'$, $X_2'$, $Y_1'$, and $Y_2'$ are measured indicators of the true variables. More specifically, $X_1'$ is the husband's report of his own party identification and $X_2'$ is his wife's report of *his* partisanship. Similarly, $Y_1'$ is the wife's report of her own identification and $Y_2'$ is her husband's report of *her* partisanship. Unlike Figure 21, we do not assume that each indicator is equally reliable; that is, we do not assign identical coefficients to the linkages between the true and the measured variables. The crucial assumptions made in the figure are that the measurement error terms (represented by $u_1$, $u_2$, $v_1$, and $v_2$) are uncorrelated with each other and with the true variables.

### TABLE 4
#### Party Identification Correlations Corrected for the Attenuating Effects of Random Measurement Error by Means of an Observations Over Time Strategy and a Multiple Indicators Approach

Observations over time

| Party Identification Pairing | Measured (observed) Correlations | True (corrected) Correlations[a] | True (corrected) Correlations[b] |
|---|---|---|---|
| 1956–1958 | .843 | .948 | .950 |
| 1958–1960 | .871 | .980 | .981 |
| 1956–1960 | .826 | .930 | .932 |

Multiple Indicators

| | Measured (observed) Correlation | True (corrected) Correlation |
|---|---|---|
| Correlation between spouses' reports of party identification | .736 | .844–.892 |

a. The corrected correlations in this column were calculated under the assumption of constant reliabilities. See Heise (1971).

b. The corrected correlations in this column were calculated under the assumption of constant error variance. See Wiley and Wiley (1971).

before too facilely treating ordinal data as interval. He also presents (1971) an example in which there is a low correspondence between the ordinal and interval scales. Thus, one must exercise some care in violating the interval assumption and be aware that in certain (usually extreme) cases, the relationship between the ordinal and interval results will be quite weak. But, in general, I would be more sanguine than some about the advantages of treating ordinal data as interval.

## SUMMATION

Throughout this paper, I have been arguing for a more causal approach to data analysis. This is certainly not a new or unique injunction, having been made previously by Alker (1969), among others. But the argument is still worth making, particularly when we still see in the social sciences many atheoretical correlational analyses that might have been handled in a more causal mode had the investigators been aware of the possibilities of causal analysis.

The best applications of causal modeling will involve an interplay between theory, research design, and data. This means that the secondary analyst may be at some disadvantage since the data are givens for him. But even for the secondary analyst, theoretical and substantive considerations must play a major role in the construction and testing of models. The very identification of a system of equations depend upon coefficient and covariance assumptions that must have some substantive grounding. As was argued earlier, one's causal analysis is more likely to go astray because of problems in the research process prior to the data analysis stage; the analysis techniques themselves are fairly straightforward and can often be found in various social science computer packages such as BMD, OSIRIS and SPSS. Among the prior problems that one must surmount are the proper specification of models, often in areas where there is little solid theory upon which to build, and the satisfactory operationalization of key concepts. It was not our aim here to go into strategies of model construction and operationalization except to say that the results of one's causal analysis are only as valid as the initial decisions made in building the model and operationalizing the variables. Even where we cannot solve such problems or satisfy certain assumptions, causal thinking and the construction of arrow diagrams may still make a significant contribution to theory building and hypothesis generation.

Thus, causal data analysis by social scientists can and should be upgraded. There is little reason to test arrows when path estimation can be done; likewise, there is no need to confine oneself to recursive models out of fears of the complexity of nonrecursive analysis. The move toward greater sophistication in data analysis does not require advanced training in econometric estimation techniques; a solid foundation in and understanding of the basic regression model along with an awareness of the properties of various estimation techniques would suffice to expand the analysis horizons of most social scientists.

Important theoretical work in causal modeling is currently being done, particularly by sociologists and economists. In addition, there are more publication outlets for methodological research such as the *Sociological Methodology* and *Political Methodology* series. The problem is that little attempt is made to present this work in terms that the layman might comprehend and thereby exploit. This results in a gap between what can be done in data analysis and what is actually being done. Political scientists reflected this gap in their heavy reliance on the Simon-Blalock technique; several readable articles on path analysis as well as curriculum developments helped narrow the gap. There still remains a substantial disparity between what can be done with nonrecursive modeling and what is actually being done. Social scientists should not be content with this situation.

## NOTES

1. The word "impose" was deliberately chosen, for it is often the case that we can assign a temporal ordering between two variables on substantive grounds even though a single time point cross-sectional design was used to obtain the measurements. A distinction should be made between the time sequence of the variables themselves and the temporal properties involved in the collection of data on the variables. For an elaboration of the point, see Hyman (1955: 193-199).

2. I do not wish to overly simplify the issues involved in causality and causal thinking. The reader should keep in mind the following caveats concerning causal analysis. First, the techniques to be discussed in this paper are appropriate only when certain key assumptions are met. Second, it is very easy to slip into using causal terminology when it is not appropriate. In most social science research, we are not working in an experimental mode in which independent variables are literally controlled and varied so that we might observe their causal impact on dependent variables. Instead, we are more often in the situation of working with independent variables that have already occurred and examining their relationships with the dependent variables of interest. If we are not careful, we may be tempted to conclude incorrectly that independent variables statistically related to dependent variables are in fact causal antecedents even though the independent variables have not actually been controlled and even though other independent variables may have comparable statistical relationships with the dependent variables. For a discussion of this problem, see Kerlinger (1974) on ex post facto research.

3. Kish (1959) considers four types of variables that may serve as sources of variation in some dependent variable; the latter two types—uncontrolled confounding variables (class III) and uncontrolled variables treated as randomized error (class IV)—are most problematic for causal inferences. Kish then discusses the role of randomization in converting class III variables to class IV and the place of tests of significance in distinguishing between the effects of class IV variables and basic explanatory variables.

4. Some investigators write an equation for $X_1$ such as $X_1 = p_{1a}R_a$ which indicates that $X_1$ is influenced by unmeasured residual variables. But for most of our purposes, this equation is unnecessary since we are not concerned with the causes of $X_1$; we cannot regress infinitely to ultimate causes. Whatever the effects of $R_a$, they are channeled through $X_1$ to the remainder of the system. Including an equation for each exogenous variable becomes useful when one estimates the unknown coefficients by multiplying pairs of equations together, taking expected values, and solving, and when one examines a matrix of coefficients to determine whether a system of equations is recursive. (See note 5 for this latter situation.)

5. A more formal way of determining whether a system of equations is recursive is to write the structural equations (including equations for the exogenous variables) with the residual terms isolated on one side of the expression and then examine the matrix of coefficients of the variables on the other side of the expression. If an upper right (or lower left depending upon the subscript notation used) matrix of zeroes results, this indicates a recursive system of equations. This can be illustrated by turning to the structural equations presented for the Miller and Stokes model in the text. Rewriting these equations so as to isolate the residual terms, and including an equation for $X_1$, we get the following revised system of equations:

$$X_1 \qquad\qquad\qquad = p_{1a}R_a \qquad\qquad [1]$$

$$-p_{21}X_1 + \quad X_2 - p_{23}X_3 \qquad = p_{2u}R_u \qquad\qquad [2]$$

$$-p_{31}X_1 - p_{32}X_2 + \quad X_3 \quad = p_{3v}R_v \qquad\qquad [3]$$

$$-p_{42}X_2 - p_{43}X_3 + X_4 = p_{4w}R_w \qquad\qquad [4]$$

The matrix of coefficients for these equations is:

$$
\begin{array}{cccc}
X_1 & X_2 & X_3 & X_4
\end{array}
$$

$$
\begin{bmatrix}
1 & 0 & 0 & 0 \\
-p_{21} & 1 & -p_{23} & 0 \\
-p_{31} & -p_{32} & 1 & 0 \\
0 & -p_{42} & -p_{43} & 1
\end{bmatrix}
\begin{array}{c}
[1] \\
[2] \\
[3] \\
[4]
\end{array}
$$

Note that all the elements above the main diagonal are not zero; hence we do not have a recursive system. Had $-p_{23}$ been replaced by a zero, the system of equations would have been recursive.

6. Linear independent equations refer to a system of equations in which none of the equations are linear combinations of the others. If one equation is a linear combination of the others, this means that the equation does not provide any independent information that can be used in solving for the unknowns in the equation system. For example, the following system of three equations in three unknowns may appear to have a unique solution for the unknowns X, Y, and Z. Observe, however, that the third equation is simply the sum of the first two (and hence a linear combination of the first two) and therefore does not provide us with any information toward a unique solution. Thus, we are actually dealing here with a situation of two equations in three unknowns which does not have a unique solution. The reader can verify for himself or herself that the following equations do not yield a unique solution.

$$X + 4Y - 3Z = 17 \qquad\qquad [1]$$

$$2X - 3Y + \quad Z = 15 \qquad\qquad [2]$$

$$3X + \quad Y - 2Z = 32 \qquad\qquad [3]$$

7. As an example of how tedious this equation can be, assume that we want to decompose the correlation $r_{34}$ in Figure 10. With respect to the formula, i refers to $X_4$, j to $X_3$ and k refers to $X_2$ and $X_3$. Thus

$$r_{34} = \sum_{k=2,3} p_{ik}r_{jk} = p_{42}r_{32} + p_{43}r_{33} = p_{42}r_{32} + p_{43}.$$

Note that we still have the term $r_{32}$ included in the decomposition of $r_{34}$. This means that we would have to use the formula once more in order to express $r_{32}$ in terms of simple and compound paths. The reader can see how quickly this procedure can become lengthy and time consuming.

8. For a more detailed discussion of the transmission of party identification across three generations, see Beck and Jennings (1975).

9. Associated with any square (n x n) matrix is a scalar quantity called a determinant. For example, if the matrix A is

$$\begin{bmatrix} 2 & 1 \\ 4 & 3 \end{bmatrix}.$$

then the determinant of A, symbolized by det A or $|A|$ is

$$\begin{vmatrix} 2 & 1 \\ 4 & 3 \end{vmatrix}$$

and is evaluated as follows. Det A = 2x3 − 4x1 = 2. In general, a 2 x 2 determinant is equal to the product of the major diagonal elements minus the product of the minor diagonal elements. The evaluation of determinants of order higher than 2 x 2 is straightforward.

Without going extensively into linear algebra, let me suggest why determinants are relevant to systems of equations. Consider the following system of two equations in two unknowns:

$$2x - 3y = 5$$
$$x - 4y = 1$$

The matrix of coefficients associated with the unknowns is

$$\begin{bmatrix} 2 & 3 \\ 1 & -4 \end{bmatrix}$$

and the determinant equals −11. In general, the presence of a non-zero determinant indicates that there is a unique solution to the unknowns, while a zero determinant indicates that there is no such solution. For example, consider the following two equations in two unknowns:

$$2x - y = 4$$
$$6x - 3y = 12$$

Here the determinant associated with the matrix of coefficients is zero. Note in fact that these two equations are linearly dependent, one being a multiple of the other, and hence do not have a unique solution.

10. For example, with $X_5$ and $X_6$ included, the matrix of coefficients becomes:

$$\begin{bmatrix} -p_{21} & 1 & -p_{23} & 0 & -p_{25} & 0 \\ -p_{31} & -p_{32} & 1 & 0 & 0 & -p_{36} \\ 0 & -p_{42} & -p_{43} & 1 & 0 & 0 \end{bmatrix}$$

If we wanted to check equation 3.22 for the rank condition, we would look to see whether we could find a non-zero 2 x 2 determinant in the matrix of coefficients after we eliminated the row of coefficients associated with equation 3.22 and eliminated the coefficients in each column where equation 3.22 had a non-zero element. If we follow these steps, we are left with the determinant

$$\begin{vmatrix} 0 & -p_{36} \\ 1 & 0 \end{vmatrix}$$

which equals $p_{36}$. Hence, equation 3.22 satisfies the rank condition. Likewise, if we eliminate the appropriate coefficients for equation 3.23, we are left with the determinant

$$\begin{vmatrix} 0 & -p_{25} \\ 1 & 0 \end{vmatrix}$$

which equals $p_{25}$; hence equation 3.23 is identified. The reader can verify for himself that application of the rank condition to equation 3.24 results in a number of 2 x 2 determinants found in the matrix of coefficients after the appropriate coefficients are eliminated. This means that equation 3.24 is overidentified.

# REFERENCES

ALKER, H. R., Jr. (1969) "Statistics and politics: the need for causal data analysis," pp. 244-313 in S. M. Lipset (ed.) Politics and the Social Sciences. New York: Oxford Univ. Press.

——— (1965) Mathematics and Politics. New York: Macmillan.

ASHER, H. B. (1974) "Some consequences of measurement error in survey data." Amer. J. of Pol. Sci. 18 (May): 469-485.

BECK, P. A. and M. K. JENNINGS (1975) "Parents as 'middlepersons' in political socialization." J. of Politics 37 (February): 83-107.

BLALOCK, H. M., Jr. (1968) "Theory building and causal inferences," pp. 155-198 in H. M. Blalock and A. B. Blalock (eds.) Methodology in Social Research. New York: McGraw-Hill.

——— (1967) "Causal inference, closed populations, and measures of association." Amer. Pol. Sci. Rev. 61 (March): 130-136.

——— (1965) "Theory building and the statistical concept of interaction." Amer. Soc. Rev. 30 (June): 374-380.

——— (1964) Causal Inferences in Nonexperimental Research. Chapel Hill: Univ. of North Carolina Press.

——— (1963) "Correlated independent variables: the problem of multicollinearity." Amer. J. of Sociology 42: 233-237.

———, C. S. WELLS, and L. F. CARTER (1970) "Statistical estimation with random measurement error," pp. 75-103 in E. F. Borgatta and G. W. Bohrnstedt (eds.) Sociological Methodology 1970. San Francisco: Jossey-Bass.

BOHRNSTEDT, G. W. and T. M. CARTER (1971) "Robustness in regression analysis," pp. 118-146 in H. L. Costner (eds.) Sociological Methodology 1971. San Francisco: Jossey-Bass.

BOUDON, R. (1968) "A new look at correlation analysis," pp. 199-235 in H. M. Blalock and A. B. Blalock (eds.) Methodology in Social Research. New York: McGraw-Hill.

CHRIST, C. (1966) Econometric Models and Methods. New York: Wiley.

COSTNER, H. L. (1971) "Theory, deduction, and rules of correspondence," pp. 299-326 in H. M. Blalock (ed.) Causal Models in the Social Sciences. Chicago: Aldine-Atherton.

DAWSON, R. and J. ROBINSON (1963) "Inter-party competition, economic variables, and welfare policies in the American states." J. of Politics 25 (May): 256-289.

DEEGAN, J. (1972) "The effects of multicollinearity and specification error on models of political behavior." Ph.D. dis. Univ. of Michigan.

DUNCAN, O. D. (1970) "Partials, partitions, and paths," pp. 38-47 in E. F. Borgatta and G. W. Bohrnstedt (eds.) Sociological Methodology 1970. San Francisco: Jossey-Bass.

––– (1969) "Some linear models for two-wave, two-variable panel analysis." Psychological Bul. 77: 177-182.

––– (1966) Path analysis: sociological examples." Amer. J. of Sociology 72: 1-16.

–––, A. O. HALLER, and A. PORTES (1971) "Peer influences on aspirations: a reinterpretation," pp. 219-244 in H. M. Blalock, Jr. (ed.) Causal Models in the Social Sciences. Chicago: Aldine-Atherton.

FARRAR, D. E. and R. R. GLAUBER (1967) "Multicollinearity in regression analysis: the problem revisited." Rev. of Economics and Statistics 49: 92-107.

FISHER, F. F. (1971) "The choice of instrumental variables in the estimation of economy-wide econometric models," pp. 245-272 in H. M. Blalock, Jr. (ed.) Causal Models in the Social Sciences. Chicago: Aldine-Atherton.

FORBES, H. D. and E. R. TUFTE (1968) "A note of caution in causal modeling." Amer. Pol. Sci. Rev. 62 (December): 1258-1264.

GOLDBERG, A. (1966) "Discerning a causal pattern among data on voting behavior," pp. 33-48 in H. M. Blalock, Jr. (ed.) Causal Models in the Social Sciences. Chicago: Aldine-Atherton.

GOLDBERGER, A. S. (1970) "On Boudon's method of linear causal analysis." Amer. Soc. Rev. 25: 97-101.

GOODMAN, L. A. (1973) "Causal analysis of data from panel studies and other kinds of surveys." Amer. J. of Sociology 78 (March): 1135-1191.

––– (1972) "A general model for the analysis of surveys." Amer. J. of Sociology 77 (May): 1035-1086.

––– (1970) "The multivariate analysis of qualitative data: interactions among multiple classifications." J. of the Amer. Statistical Assn. 65: 225-256.

HAUSER, R. M. and A. S. GOLDBERGER (1971) "The treatment of unobservable variables in path analysis," pp. 81-117 in H. L. Costner (ed.) Sociological Methodology 1971. San Francisco: Jossey-Bass.

HAYS, W. L. (1963) Statistics for Psychologists. New York: Holt, Rinehart & Winston.

HEISE, D. R. (1971) "Separating reliability and stability in test-retest correlation," pp. 348-363 in H. M. Blalock (ed.) Causal Models in the Social Sciences. Chicago: Aldine-Atherton.

——— (1970) "Causal inference from panel data," pp. 3-27 in E. F. Borgatta and G. W. Bohrnstedt (eds.) Sociological Methodology 1970. San Francisco: Jossey-Bass.

HIBBS, D. A., Jr. (1974) "Problems of statistical estimation and causal inference in time-series regression models," pp. 252-308 in H. L. Costner (ed.) Sociological Methodology 1973-1974. San Francisco: Jossey-Bass.

HYMAN, H. (1955) Survey Design and Analysis. New York: Free Press.

KARNS, D. (1974) "The choice of estimation techniques for nonrecursive models." (mimeo)

——— (1973) "Interdependent political systems." (mimeo)

KERLINGER, F. N. (1964) Foundations of Behavioral Research. New York: Holt, Rinehart & Winston.

KEY, V. O. (1949) Southern Politics. New York: Knopf.

KISH, L. (1959) "Some statistical problems in research design." Amer. Soc. Rev. 24 (June): 328-338.

LABOVITZ, S. (1970) "The assignment of numbers to rank order categories." Amer. Soc. Rev. 35 (June): 515-524.

——— (1967) "Some observations on measurement and statistics." Social Forces 46 (December): 151-160.

LAND, K. C. (1973) "Identification, parameter estimation, and hypothesis testing in recursive sociological models," pp. 19-49 in A. S. Goldberger and O. D. Duncan (eds.) Structural Equation Models in the Social Sciences. New York: Seminar Press.

——— (1970) "On the estimation of path coefficients for unmeasured variables from correlations among observed variables." Social Forces 48: 506-511.

——— (1969) "Principles of path analysis," pp. 3-37 in E. Borgatta (ed.) Sociological Methodology 1969. San Francisco: Jossey-Bass.

LEHNEN, R. G. and G. G. KOCH (1974) "A general linear approach to the analysis of nonmetric data: applications for political science." Amer. J. of Pol. Sci. 18 (May): 283-313.

——— (1973) "A comparison of categorical and conventional regression techniques in political analysis." Paper presented at the 69th annual meeting of Amer. Pol. Sci. Assn., September 4-8, New Orleans.

LOCKARD, D. (1959) New England State Politics. Princeton: Princeton Univ. Press.

MAYER, L. S. (1971) "A note on treating ordinal data as interval data." Amer. Soc. Rev. (June): 519-520.

——— (1970) "Comment on 'The assignment of numbers to rank order categories.'" Amer. Soc. Rev. 35 (August): 916-917.

MILLER, W. E. and D. E. STOKES (1966) "Constituency influence in Congress," pp. 351-372 in A. Campbell et al. Elections and the Political Order. New York: Wiley.

PELZ, D. C. and F. M. ANDREWS (1964) "Detecting causal priorities in panel study data." Amer. Soc. Rev. 29: 836-848.

RABINOWITZ, S. M. (1969) "Socialization within the family: a reciprocal causal model." (mimeo)

SELLTIZ, C. et al. (1959) Research Methods in Social Relations. New York: Holt, Rinehart & Winston.

SIEGEL, P. M. and R. W. HODGE (1968) "A causal approach to the study of measurement error," pp. 28-59 in H. M. Blalock and A. B. Blalock (eds.) Methodology in Social Research. New York: McGraw Hill.

SIMON, H. (1957) "Spurious correlation: a causal interpretation," pp. 37-49 in Models of Man. New York: Wiley.

STOKES, D. E. (1974) "Compound paths: an expository note." Amer. J. of Pol. Sci. 18 (February): 191-214.

STROUSE, J. and J. O. WILLIAMS (1972) "A non-additive model for state policy research." J. of Politics 34 (May): 648-657.

TUKEY, J. W. (1954) "Causation, regression, and path analysis," pp. 35-66 in O. Kempthorne et al. (eds.) Statistics and Mathematics in Biology. Ames: Iowa State College Press.

TURNER, M. E. and C. D. STEVENS (1959) "The regression analysis of causal paths." Biometrics 15 (June): 236-258.

USLANER, E. M. (1976) Regression Analysis: Simultaneous Equation Estimation. In this series.

VAN METER, D. S. and H. B. ASHER (1973) "Causal analysis: its promise for policy studies." Policy Studies J. 2 (Winter): 103-109.

WERTS, C. E., K. G. JORESKOG, and R. L. LINN (1973) "Identification and estimation in path analysis with unmeasured variables." Amer. J. of Sociology 78 (May): 1469-1484.

WILEY, D. E. (1973) "The identification problem for structural equation models with unmeasured variables," pp. 69-83 in A. S. Goldberger and O. D. Duncan (eds.) Structural Equation Models in the Social Sciences. New York: Seminar Press.

― ― ― and J. A. WILEY (1971) "The estimation of measurement error in panel data," pp. 364-373 in H. M. Blalock (ed.) Causal Models in the Social Sciences. Chicago: Aldine-Atherton.

WILSON, T. P. (1971) "Critique of ordinal variables," pp. 415-431 in H. M. Blalock (ed.) Causal Models in the Social Sciences. Chicago: Aldine-Atherton.

WONNACOTT, R. J. and T. H. WONNACOTT (1970) Econometrics. New York: Wiley.

WRIGHT, S. (1960) "Path coefficients and path regressions: alternative or complementary concepts?" Biometrics 16 (June): 189-202.

― ― ― (1934) "The method of path coefficients." Annals of Math. Statistics 5 (September): 161-215.

# APPENDIX A

## Standardized Variables and Mathematical Expectation

Any set of data can be put in standard form (that is, given a mean of zero and a standard deviation of one) by the following simple transformation. Take each original observation, subtract from it the mean of the observations, and divide by the standard deviation. If this is done for each datum, the new set of observations will have a mean of zero and a standard deviation of one.

For example, assume that we have the following three data points or observations: 5, 1, and 3. The mean of these three observations is obviously 3 and the standard deviation is 2.

$$\text{Standard deviation} = \sqrt{\frac{\sum_{i=1}^{n} (x_i - \bar{X})^2}{n - 1}}$$

$$= \sqrt{\frac{(5-3)^2 + (1-3)^2 + (3-3)^2}{3-1}} = 2$$

If we subtract the mean from each observation and divide by the standard deviation, we get the three data points of 1, −1, and 0 as shown below. The reader can verify for himself that these observations have a mean of zero and a standard deviation of one.

| Original Observations $(x_i)$ | Original minus mean $(x_i - \bar{X})$ | Original minus mean divided by the standard deviation $\dfrac{x_i - \bar{X}}{\text{s.d.}}$ |
|---|---|---|
| 5 | 2 | 1 |
| 1 | −2 | −1 |
| 3 | 0 | 0 |

Mathematical expectation is defined for both the continuous and discrete cases, although we are concerned here only with the latter. In the discrete case, the expected value of X where X is some random variable is symbolized by $E(X)$, and defined as

$$E(X) = \sum_X Xp(X).$$

This expression means that we sum over X outcomes or observations, weighting each outcome or observation by its associated probability. Before explaining these terms, let me try to present to the reader an intuitive meaning of expected value.

Imagine that there is a lottery in which 100 tickets have been sold for $1 each, the payoff for winning the lottery is $50, and that a person has bought one ticket. The question that we might ask is: what is the person's expected gain or loss in playing this lottery? Relating our definition of expected value to the present example, we would say that the lottery has two possible outcomes for the purchaser of one ticket—he could win $50 (disregarding the cost of the ticket) or lose $1. Each of these outcomes has a probability associated with it—he could win the lottery with a probability of $1/100$ since he bought one of the 100 lottery tickets, or he could lose the lottery with a probability of $99/100$. Relating these numbers to our definition of expected value, we would say that the $E(X)$, one's expected gain or loss in playing the lottery is

$$E(X) = \sum_{\substack{X=\$50, \\ -\$1}} Xp(X) = (\$50)\left(\frac{1}{100}\right) + (-\$1)\left(\frac{99}{100}\right) = -\$.49.$$

This result means that if a person played the lottery, he or she could expect to lose 49 cents. The reader might very well ask how a person could lose 49 cents since in any single play of the lottery one either wins $50 or loses $1. The answer is that if one played the lottery a large number of times, the average outcome for each time it was played would be a loss of 49 cents. Thus, an expected value is an average outcome or average value.

We make use of mathematical expectation and standardized variables in many of the derivations presented in this paper so the reader should carefully examine the following material. Assume that we have n pairs of observations on two variables, X and Y. For example, we might have sampled n individuals and collected information on their level of education (X) and their level of political interest (Y). Or we might have sampled n counties and gathered data on the percent Catholic (X) and the percent Democratic (Y) in each county. Symbolically, we might refer to these data points as $x_1, x_2, \ldots, x_n$ which would represent the n observations on the X variable and $y_1, y_2, \ldots, y_n$, the n observations on the Y variable.

If the observations have been collected by a random sampling scheme, then the probability of any $x_i y_i$ is $1/n$. By the definition of expected value then

$$E(XY) = \sum_{XY} XYp(X,Y) = \sum_{i=1}^{n} x_i y_i p(x_i, y_i) = \frac{\sum_{i=1}^{n} x_i y_i}{n}.$$

The correlation between X and Y can be expressed as

$$r_{XY} = \frac{\text{cov}(X,Y)}{s_X s_Y} = \frac{\dfrac{\sum\limits_{i=1}^{n} (x_i - \bar{X})(y_i - \bar{Y})}{n}}{\sqrt{\dfrac{\sum\limits_{i=1}^{n} (x_i - \bar{X})^2}{n-1}} \sqrt{\dfrac{\sum\limits_{i=1}^{n} (y_i - \bar{Y})^2}{n-1}}}$$

If our variables are standardized, then the denominator of the correlation coefficient becomes unity, $\bar{X}$ and $\bar{Y}$ equal zero, and the entire expression simplifies to

$$r_{XY} = \frac{\sum\limits_{i=1}^{n} x_i y_i}{n}.$$

Note from above that $E(XY)$ also equals

$$\frac{\sum\limits_{i=1}^{n} x_i y_i}{n}.$$

Hence, this means that the expected value of the product of two standardized variables ($E(XY)$) is equal to the correlation between them, a result that will be used extensively. For example, if we assume that two standardized variables are uncorrelated, an alternative way of expressing this assumption is to assert that the expected value of their product equals zero. In addition, the expected value of the square of a standardized variable, $E(X^2)$, equals unity. In fact, the $E(X^2)$ is the variance of X, and since X is standardized its standard deviation and variance are equal to one.

For additional information about mathematical expectation, see Appendix B in *Statistics* (1963) by William Hays.

## APPENDIX B

### Solutions for $p_{31}$ and $p_{32}$ in the Model of Figure 6

$$X_3 = p_{31}X_1 + p_{32}X_2 + p_{3v}R_v$$

Multiply the above equation by the instruments $X_1$ and $X_2$:

$$X_1X_3 = p_{31}X_1^2 + p_{32}X_1X_2 + p_{3v}X_1R_v$$

$$X_2X_3 = p_{31}X_1X_2 + p_{32}X_2^2 + p_{3v}X_2R_v$$

Take the expected value of each equation, recalling that the expected value of the product of two standardized variables is their correlation and the expected value of the square of a standardized variable is its variance which is unity. Further recall that $X_1$ and $X_2$ are assumed to be uncorrelated with $R_v$. We then obtain the following system of two equations in the two unknowns $p_{31}$ and $p_{32}$:

$$r_{13} = p_{31} + p_{32}r_{12}$$

$$r_{23} = p_{31}r_{12} + p_{32}$$

The solutions are:

$$p_{31} = \frac{r_{13} - r_{12}r_{23}}{1 - r_{12}^2}$$

$$p_{32} = \frac{r_{23} - r_{12}r_{13}}{1 - r_{12}^2}$$

## APPENDIX C

### The Decomposition of the Correlations in the Recursive Representation Model of Figure 10

$$r_{12} = p_{21}$$

$$r_{13} = p_{31} + p_{21}p_{32}$$

$$r_{14} = p_{21}p_{42} + p_{31}p_{43} + p_{21}p_{32}p_{43}$$

$$r_{23} = p_{32} + p_{21}p_{31}$$

$$r_{24} = p_{42} + p_{32}p_{43} + p_{21}p_{31}p_{43}$$

$$r_{34} = p_{43} + p_{32}p_{42} + p_{31}p_{21}p_{42}$$

Note that the decomposition of $r_{34}$ does not have the additional term $p_{31}p_{21}p_{32}p_{43}$. This term would violate Wright's rule about no path passing through the same variable more than once since it would be going through $X_3$ twice.